DIANA

THE SECRETS OF HER STYLE

NA

THE SECRETS OF HER STYLE

BY DIANE CLEHANE

GT
PUBLISHING

Additional acknowledgments and picture credits are on pages 156-159.

Published in 1998 by GT Publishing Corporation
16 E. 40th Street
New York, NY 10016

Library of Congress Cataloging-in-Publication Data
Clehane, Diane
   Diana: the secrets of her style / by Diane Clehane
     p. cm.
   ISBN 1-57719-348-2 (hardcover)
   1. Diana, Princess of Wales, 1961- –Clothing. 2. Fashion–
   Great Britain–History–20th century. 3. Princesses–Great
   Britain–Biography. I.Title
   DA591.A45D5294 1998
   941.085'092–dc21
     [b]   98-20362
                                                       CIP

ISBN: 1-57719-348-2

Printed in the United States

10 9 8 7 6 5 4 3 2 1

First Printing

CONTENTS

DIANA
FASHIONING A LEGEND

DIANA, PRINCESS OF WALES, WAS ONE OF FASHION'S BRIGHTEST STARS. She found a way to articulate something all women instinctively know: our clothes speak more fluently—and honestly—about ourselves than words ever could. While Diana popularized pearl chokers, designer handbags and short hair, her greatest contribution to fashion was her intuitive understanding of the power of style. It was a gift she used wisely.

Diana made us believe in transformation and reinvention and she did it through the clothes she wore. Her emotional life was mirrored by her appearance. Her journey from a rather ordinary-looking kindergarten teacher to Her Royal Highness to a stunning, independent single woman was rife with images every woman could relate to. To women of all ages who grew up believing in fairy-tale endings, Diana in her unabashedly romantic wedding dress was the embodiment of a modern-day Cinderella. In her short black cocktail dress worn as "revenge dressing" to upstage her unfaithful husband and strike back at those who underestimated her, she became a role model for embattled survivors. In photographs which captured her toned body dashing off to the gym in colorful workout clothes (the same ones we own!), she represented the physical ideal of the nineties: radiantly healthy, sensual and strong.

Many of us saw our own reflection in Diana. When she exchanged ball gowns and tiaras for simple suits and straight hair, we recognized ourselves—the idealized version of ourselves—in her. We wanted to be like her, and she, it seemed, wanted to be like us. That is the essence of her appeal: Diana was Everywoman. She was an old friend who survived a husband's infidelity and a painful divorce, the death of a beloved parent, the ups and downs of fractured familial relationships and struggles with self-esteem. She used food to self-medicate, shopped out of boredom and cut her hair when her relationship soured. What woman hasn't done at least one of these things? Diana offered hope that one could emerge from personal difficulties intact and look more beautiful than ever. She showed us that not every sadness or disappointment has to leave a visible, indelible mark. Ironically, she also taught us that the scars we could not see were inevitably the deepest.

When I began researching this book, I was struck by the fact that although I had looked at literally thousands of images of Diana, I never once came upon a "bad" picture of her. Whether in formal portraits or candid shots, she radiated a vibrant, unpretentious beauty that seemed to jump right off the page. Before I became a journalist, I followed Diana with great interest through the hundreds of articles and books that had been written about her. We were the same age and shared the same nickname (friends began calling me "Lady Di" when I began emulating her early look by wearing ruffled collar blouses, pearls, red shoes and other Diana-inspired emblems). I, like most Americans, had little opportunity to hear her speak, so I came to know Diana through the clothes she wore. Years later, I was able to cross-reference the events in Diana's life with the styles she favored at the time. It was clear that she used her clothes to tell her story and to help create the various personas that captured our imagination.

In the winter of 1998, I learned just how true that assessment was. After meeting with many of the designers who dressed Diana, I came to appreciate that they knew the Princess in a way that few others did. "Her moods were very much reflected in the clothes she chose to wear," said Elizabeth Emanuel, who together with her husband, David, created what is arguably the most famous wedding dress in history. "You could see when she felt good and when she wanted to hide away. Her clothes were a kind of vocabulary for her." And when Diana became proficient in the language of clothes, she knew exactly what she wanted and from whom. Most designers worked with her for a specific period of her life until their creations no longer suited her changing tastes. Some, however, forged bonds with Diana that endured—but only because they changed with her. Each of the people interviewed for this book offer wonderfully candid insights about Diana, her style and how her life was reflected in her appearance. After spending hundreds of hours examining every aspect of Diana's style, I have an even greater admiration for her. This is due in no small part to the enormous respect and affection she elicited from those who worked with her. While Diana had to learn to develop a sense of style, her innate graciousness and humility were evident from the very beginning of her public life.

The Princess evolved from being a young British girl whose fashion sense was uneven at best into a breathtaking international figure through some very public experimentation. Diana was never shy about "working on herself," never letting us believe anything came too easily to her. She was an avid consumer—a fact that further insured her a place in our collective consciousness. She was a faithful devotee to a host of therapies and treatments designed to improve both her inner and outer selves. We worried when she seemingly teetered on the brink of being engulfed by them all, and were relieved when she inevitably changed course just in time. Part of the reason we felt—and still feel—so connected to Diana is that she elicited strong feelings of empathy, never envy. For all her glamour, style and beauty, we knew that underneath it all, she struggled just like the rest of us. Whatever her behavior, we understood and empathized with the reasons behind it.

Much has been made of the idea that Diana died at the peak of her physical beauty. But how can we really know that? Diana had not yet finished the transformation she had begun in the last year of her life. She truly became more attractive as she matured. Her looks—and her life—were a work in progress. How would she have handled growing older? Undoubtedly, she would have remained the embodiment of glamour for a generation of women as she (and they) reached the milestones of a fortieth, fiftieth and sixtieth birthday. Surely she would have shown us how to age with grace and style. "I feel cheated that I will never see another new photograph of her again," a friend confided to me when I told her that I was writing a book about the Princess's style. "It was always wonderful to see what she was doing, what she was wearing and how she coped with it all. There is nobody to take her place now."

No, there is not. The world craves glamour and Diana offered it to us in an intriguing package, combining it with a sense of purpose which made her even more beautiful. Some may argue that to write about Diana as a style icon is to trivialize her humanitarian efforts. Nothing could be further from the truth. In this increasingly telegenic age, it was the power of her beauty that enabled Diana to accomplish her humanitarian goals. She came to understand that and used it to its full advantage in the last years of her life. The Christie's auction had proven that. But even as her focus shifted, she was far from abandoning her glamorous image entirely. The week of her death, she was reportedly scheduled to have a final fitting for a Giorgio Armani gown she had planned to wear to an AIDS benefit.

Diana was a woman who never set out to become a legend—fashionable or otherwise. But her position as one of the most legendary figures of our time is assured partly because our favorite images of her are forever frozen in time. In our hearts and minds, she remains eternally young; her inner and outer beauty will never wane. But it is neither her incredible beauty nor her innate sense of style that fully defines her legacy. Diana is destined to be remembered as a stunning paradox: a woman who dreaded the scrutiny of the public but craved the attention, who abhorred formality yet shone amidst pomp and circumstance like no royal ever had. Ultimately, Diana was not a woman that could ever be completely understood. Complicated and simple, outwardly sophisticated and emotionally naive, she was—so we made ourselves believe—just like us. In truth, she was like no one else in the world.

Diane Clehane
May 1998

Diana was reportedly scheduled to have a fitting for this dress by Giorgio Armani the week of her death.

1981
The nineteen-year-old
Lady Diana Spencer
photographed by
Snowdon for British *Vogue*
in a silk blouse by Elizabeth
and David Emanuel.

1997
This portrait by Snowdon of the Princess modeling the "John Travolta dress" was taken for the Christie's auction catalog. The ink-blue velvet gown by Victor Edelstein was first worn in 1985 to the White House.

1987 & 1990

Diana often chose Terence Donovan to photograph her for official portraits. LEFT, How the fresh-faced princess often arrived for shoots, and RIGHT, looking regal and every inch the royal in a Catherine Walker beaded gown and the Queen Mary diamond tiara given to her by Queen Elizabeth in 1981.

1996
On her way to Washington, D.C., Diana exuded confidence in a chic power suit.

1997
In August, Diana seemed happy to get away from it all with Dodi Fayed on his father's yacht off the coast of Portofino.

Diana was a thoroughly modern princess whose photogenic looks made her a fashion icon for the media age. With her model's figure, she could pull off virtually any look she attempted. Her clothes were never considered cutting edge, yet as soon as she wore them they became instantly chic. She had, over time, become more sure of herself—and it showed. As Diana's style evolved, she favored more streamlined clothes for both day and evening. She clearly loved clothes and knew how to have fun with them, all the while looking quite polished and patrician.

LEFT, In a sleeveless red coatdress by Tomasz Starzewski, Diana displayed her crisp, clean, decidedly luxurious style at Wimbledon in 1994. OPPOSITE LEFT, The Princess was proud of her toned body and chose a revealing halter dress by Catherine Walker for her appearance in London at a Serpentine Gallery benefit hosted by *Vanity Fair* in 1995. CENTER, For a 1996 charity fund-raiser at Northwestern University in Chicago, Diana wore a stunning Versace gown in purple, the school's color. RIGHT, This one-shoulder silk chiffon dress with translucent beads and crystals was made for the Princess by Japanese designer Hachi in 1985. It was one of the first column-style dresses she wore—they would later become her signature—and an early indication of her affinity for modern, glamorous eveningwear.

1

A STAR IS BORN

When Lady Diana Spencer was thrust into the spotlight wearing the standard Sloane uniform of cashmere sweaters and Laura Ashley skirts, her large, expressive eyes glancing out at the world from beneath a thick fringe, no one could have foretold that she was destined to become one of the most enthralling and stylish women of our time. Looking back at the earliest photographs of this shy, slightly plump nineteen-year-old girl, it is virtually impossible to envision the beloved icon who embodied an intriguing combination of humanity and glamour in a way that no public figure had ever done before. And yet, she was completely captivating from the very beginning. She had an indefinable star quality that few people possess—she had style.

PREVIOUS PAGE, On the polo fields in her "black sheep" sweater by Warm and Wonderful, the first of many Di-inspired fashion trends. The company sold $1 million worth of the whimsical pullover.

ABOVE, Before her wedding Diana's wardrobe consisted mainly of casual clothes, like her favorite overalls.

OPPOSITE, TOP, Bellville Sassoon designed the navy sailor suit Diana wore to meet the Queen when her upcoming marriage was approved by The Privy Council in March of 1981. BOTTOM, She bought her first formal suit at Harrods for her engagement photo call.

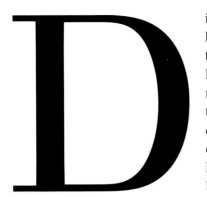

Diana followed a long-standing tradition of the British aristocracy—as a teenager her earliest fashion choices were heavily influenced by her mother, Frances Shand-Kydd, whose tastes leaned towards matronly English hats from milliner John Boyd and the conservative designs of dressmakers Bill Pashley and Donald Campbell. "She was an English girl of a certain class and experience," said Campbell, who began dressing Diana when her sister Lady Jane Fellowes brought her to his William Street shop in Knightsbridge. "She thought fashion was a necessary evil. For those people, fashion is very much down the line. They're told at a very early age, 'Don't be vain about how you look, don't look in the mirror, because no one is going to be looking at you.' It's really about that sort of attitude, and unfortunately it stays with them all their lives."

Diana was incredibly unsophisticated about fashion during those early years, and the shy vulnerability of a young woman suddenly thrust into the spotlight was reflected in the choices she made. Her wardrobe was unremarkable and demure; her simply patterned skirts were almost always too long and were worn with cotton blouses and loose-fitting jackets. After she became Princess of Wales virtually everything was topped off by small, fussy hats which aged her. "Clothes are not my priority," Diana had once insisted. But she quickly realized that her modest wardrobe of a few colorful jumpers and long skirts, jeans and just one evening gown was completely inadequate for her new role as princess-to-be. She began to shop with a vengeance for more appropriate clothes.

"It's a myth that you can advise the royal family on what to wear," said Campbell, whose clothes Diana wore up until 1986. "To be absolutely honest, she chose, I didn't advise. She just came in and started buying. I don't think there were many of the things she wore of mine that I would have chosen for her. She was totally inexperienced. No one was advising her. She bought

everything off the rails—nothing was made for her at all. All she had to go on was the established way of doing things, and I think she was frightened of appearing taller than the Prince. There was nothing 'razzle-dazzle' in the early days."

When Diana became engaged to Prince Charles in February of 1981 and a photo call was planned, it was the first time she had ever needed a formal suit. She chose (at her mother's urging) an ill-fitting, off-the-peg suit by Cojana, bought at Harrods for £310 and charged to her mother's account. Anxious that her choice be deemed respectful, Diana asked to have the skirt lengthened, making the already dowdy suit look even more matronly. The only thing flattering about the style was its royal blue color which set off her eyes. Careful not to tower over her fiancé, the 5'10" princess-to-be wore sensible low-heeled pumps for the photo call. (Somewhat difficult to find in London's many boutiques, factories began turning out a thousand pairs a week to keep up with the demand for Lady Di-inspired footwear.) The photographs taken that day served as a catalyst for Diana, who set out immediately to improve her image. At that moment, she decided she would begin losing weight and vowed to cultivate a more stylish appearance.

Diana may have chosen something decidedly understated to wear when the engagement was announced, but her choice of rings clearly demonstrated a love of fabulously extravagant jewelry. When she was presented with a tray of eight engagement rings from Garrard, the Crown Jeweller, (whose association with the royal family dates back to 1722), Diana immediately picked the largest one. It once appeared in a Garrard catalog priced at £28,500. Interestingly, the magnificent sapphire engagement ring surrounded by fourteen diamonds was not made exclusively for Diana, although it has become one of the most enduring symbols of her style. 'The Ring', as it came to be known at the time, immediately set off a major trend as women around the world began shopping for look-a-likes at a considerably lesser price.

Shortly after the engagement, Diana's sister, Lady Jane Fellowes, who had been an editorial assistant at British *Vogue*, introduced her to the magazine's editors and it was decided they would help Diana with her wardrobe and her image. Beauty editor Felicity Clark and fashion editor Anna Harvey were assigned to the task by editor Beatrix Miller. Racks and racks of clothes were sent to the *Vogue* offices by London's best-known designers, including Bruce Oldfield and Bellville Sassoon, and Diana became a frequent visitor via the back stairs to review their offerings.

This red chiffon gown with a
ruffled bodice and hem was
designed by Bellville Sassoon
for the June 1981 premiere of
For Your Eyes Only. "She
sparkled in it," said David
Sassoon.

June 1981

Bellville Sassoon

*She managed to show the world
she possessed a flair for dramatic clothes.
This proved to be the first time Diana's
sheer star power eclipsed everything
else around her.*

Although Diana was under the tutelage of the editors at British *Vogue*, she never relied exclusively on their guidance, and out of respect for Diana the magazine's editors consistently played down their role as her mentors. She still enjoyed popping into a few designer shops around London by herself or with her mother. "When she got engaged, her mother brought her in to us and asked us to make the going-away outfit," said David Sassoon of Bellville Sassoon. "The suit was partly her idea. She chose the color, which she called 'cantaloupe.' She wanted that color and she wanted it in silk. She was very particular about having a straight skirt because she thought that was very sophisticated. We made two jackets—one with long sleeves because she was worried about the weather." Diana so loved the suit that she wore it at least five different times between 1981 and 1982.

Sassoon, who also designed the navy sailor suit for Diana's first official meeting with the Queen, created over sixty styles with Belinda Bellville for her during the early eighties. The clothes mirrored Diana's sweet and sincere persona and reflected the romantic mood in fashion that was so popular during that time. "She always liked romantic clothes and pretty colors—she had a great sense of color. She understood that photographers liked color and she liked to surprise in terms of fashion. If it was something that was going to catch the press or the public's eye, she enjoyed that." One of the first evening dresses to do just that was Bellville Sassoon's red chiffon gown with embroidered silver dots that Diana wore to the London premiere of *For Your Eyes Only* in June of 1981. The corseted, full-skirted dress sparkled in front of the flashbulbs and flattered the newly slim Diana. She looked youthful and very pretty—just like a princess.

"We were asked by Anna Harvey, 'Do you have anything with a high neck that would be suitable—something romantic—for an important client?' She couldn't tell me who the person was," recalled Elizabeth Emanuel of the first time she and her then-husband and partner, David, were asked to send clothes to Vogue House on Hanover Square for

Diana made headlines in this revealing black taffeta gown by Elizabeth and David Emanuel at her first formal evening engagement with Prince Charles in March of 1981.

Diana's consideration. "We happened to have this silk chiffon blouse with a satin bow and a pale pink skirt that went with it. It wasn't until later on that we knew it had been for Diana." The Emanuel blouse, with its frilly piecrust neckline, was chosen for a formal debutante portrait taken by Lord Snowdon which appeared in British *Vogue.* Afterwards, Diana asked Anna Harvey for the phone number of the up-and-coming designers so she could go and see the rest of their collection.

Diana was in search of something to wear for her first formal evening engagement with Prince Charles when she visited the Emanuels. A low-cut, strapless and sequined black silk taffeta dress that hung on a rack in their workroom caught her eye immediately. "It was a sample," said Elizabeth Emanuel. "She tried it on and we thought she looked really lovely in it–very different than how she had been seen before. Up until that point, people had only seen her in her Sloaney clothes. But we didn't anticipate it would cause such a huge stir. It was the most grown-up and sophisticated dress she had ever worn." The sight of Diana spilling out of the revealing gown as she and Prince Charles stepped from the car at Goldsmith's Hall in March of 1981 caused a sensation in newspapers all over Britain. (Diana never made the same mistake twice when it came to her clothes. From that point on, when alighting from cars she adopted the ladylike gesture of covering her décolletage with her hands or her handbag.) Whether or not she had knowingly selected the dress to set herself apart from the dowdy fashion image that the other royals had, she managed to show the world she possessed a flair for choosing and wearing dramatic clothes. This occasion proved to be the first in a lifetime of events where Diana's sheer star power would eclipse everyone–and every-thing–around her. "Photos of her came out the same day the budget had been announced, and that got moved to the middle pages," said Emanuel. "She was on the cover of every newspaper in London." As for the dress, unlike many of the other items in her wardrobe that were acquired at the time, Diana never wore it again.

Diana's wedding dress by the Emanuels featured a 25-foot train, 44 yards of ivory silk taffeta and 10,000 mother-of-pearl sequins and pearls.

Despite the mixed reviews Diana had received for wearing the Emanuels' evening dress, she chose the husband and wife team to design her wedding dress. It was first thought that dressmaker Bill Pashley (who had designed both her sisters' wedding dresses) would be chosen for the coveted assignment of creating Diana's dress, but it was the Emanuels who were awarded the job.

In the spring of 1981, they began the momentous task in earnest. As Diana sat cross-legged on the floor of their Brook Street studio reviewing possible designs, she became enthralled by one dress she saw on a model. "I want that dress," she declared. But the Emanuels believed that Diana needed something created especially for her, not something from their current collection. "She tried on the dress she saw just to get a feel about how it would look and she really liked the shape, so we decided to model the dress on that dress. It had the big frills and the tiny waist that she liked."

As the wedding day neared, keeping the design of the dress a secret proved more and more difficult. Elizabeth Emanuel was constantly bombarded with phone calls from over-zealous fashion editors who did everything from cajole to threaten her for a description of the dress. "We had a code of secrecy. Everyone was hounding us for details. We actually made another dress just in case it got found out. I got absolutely paranoid," said Emanuel, who began discarding decoy white fabric in the trash while burning unused scraps of ivory silk from the actual dress at the end of each work day. "We tried to take every precaution but we had no help from the Palace. I very much felt that with Diana it was the same. We were a team, in it together."

"I think she looked her most beautiful. For just that day, things seemed to be right."

The pressure of preparing for her wedding had clearly taken its toll on Diana. At the start of the fittings, she had been a British size 14 but she had lost 20 pounds since work on the dress had begun. On her wedding day she had a 22-inch waist and was down to a size 10. "She lost loads and loads of weight and went through some pretty drastic changes," said Emanuel. "It was a problem, but I think she looked more and more beautiful." When the day finally came, Emanuel remembers Diana looking absolutely radiant. Barbara Daly was hired to apply a minimum amount of makeup and completed the task in just 45 minutes. Kevin Shanley from Head Lines, Diana's favorite hair salon at the time, had a more daunting task. He tried, without much success, to alter Diana's regular style to accommodate the Spencer tiara by

brushing her heavy fringe to one side. "We were all at Clarence House to help her get ready," said Emanuel. "We were all watching the television coverage and we could hear the people on the Mall and it was like a stereo effect." Diana giggled while watching the programs with rapt attention. "It was quite fun because we all knew what the dress would look like and all the commentators were talking about it. There were Corgis everywhere and Diana was singing away. She was very happy that day."

The House of Emanuel had become known for designing very romantic clothes and Diana's dress was certainly no exception. "We wanted to make something really extravagant," said Emanuel. "We wanted to make a long train, longer than those in any other royal wedding that had come before." The paper-taffeta bridal gown was fashioned from 44 yards of ivory-

OPPOSITE, Bellville Sassoon designed much of Diana's trousseau, including this cantaloupe-colored suit she wore as her going-away outfit.

RIGHT, Diana wore an off-the-peg white gabardine coat by Donald Campbell with a printed silk crepe de chine dress from the designer on the first day of her honeymoon aboard the Britannia.

The sweet, unpretentious young girl who had married her prince was embarking on a series of dramatic transformations

At Balmoral in August of 1981, Diana greeted photographers in a sporty two-piece houndstooth checked suit by her mother's dressmaker Bill Pashley.

colored silk taffeta. It featured a 25-foot train and 10,000 mother-of-pearl sequins and pearls that were hand embroidered on the dress by Elizabeth and her mother ("We all chipped in to finish the job"). The unabashedly ornate design was a frothy meringue of frills, bows and ruffles that incorporated all of the oldest bridal traditions. "Something old" was the lace used on the central panel once worn by Queen Mary. A Nottingham firm had been hired by the Emanuels to design the lace that would go around the rest of the dress. The "new" silk was spun at England's only silk farm, Lullingstone. (They were unable to produce all that was needed to complete the dress. "But at least we were able to get some in there," said Emanuel.) "Borrowed" was the Spencer family tiara (the Emanuels covered its underside in brown velvet) and her mother's diamond drop earrings. A tiny "blue" bow had been sewn into the waistband and a good luck charm, an 18-carat yellow-gold horseshoe studded with white diamonds, was stitched onto the back of the dress. The ivory tulle veil that glittered with thousands of hand-sewn sequins shaded Diana's blushing face. Her shoes, made by Clive Shilton, were low-heeled, covered with lacy rosettes and adorned with embroidery that mirrored the style of the dress.

When Diana emerged Cinderella-like from her glass coach at St. Paul's on July 29, 1981, she resembled a butterfly breaking out of its chrysalis. It was exactly what Elizabeth Emanuel had envisioned. Surrounded in a bilious cloud of lace and taffeta, Diana looked every inch a princess. The ride to the church had caused the

dress to wrinkle slightly, but it was not the fashion disaster some reported it to be. "Too costumey and overly fussy," claimed some fashion critics. (Diana seemed not to take the criticism too much to heart. That year, she selected a photograph from the wedding for her Christmas card.) The dress, with its fitted and boned bodice and crinoline skirt, epitomized the romantic styles so popular at the time. Diana was, in fact, the embodiment of millions of women's hopes and dreams for a fairy-tale existence, and never more so than when she walked down that 652-foot red carpet to the altar. She personified a romantic ideal: a kindergarten teacher whose shy smile summed up the universal female fantasy of marrying a "prince." And while her wedding dress was certainly nothing like what she might have chosen had she gotten the chance to marry again, its ethereal quality seemed ideally suited to the nineteen-year-old girl who loved Barbara Cartland novels and was embarking on what she hoped would be the greatest romantic adventure of her life. Diana's wedding gown had a huge impact on the bridal industry, which began producing a myriad of look-alike Victorian-style dresses while heralding a 'return to romance.' Within days it inspired a host of copycat versions around the world.

"When I look back at the wedding and see her on her wedding day, there were some things—maybe you could say her hair wasn't quite right or the dress had some creases. . .but sometimes it's those things that make it magical because she was human. Whatever criticisms were handed out about the dress, I just think she

ABOVE, Diana's presence thrilled the crowds in Wales during her first visit in October of 1981. The Donald Campbell suit in the Welsh national colors struck just the right note.

LEFT, Diana watched the Highland Games at Braemar dressed in a tam-o'-shanter and plaid dress by Caroline Charles.

While Diana's eveningwear drew rave reviews, like this Bruce Oldfield blue silk chiffon gown, OPPOSITE, worn with silver accessories in 1983, her daywear choices were often a bit fussy but charming nonetheless. LEFT, For her first trip to Ascot in 1981, she wore this red silk two-piece suit with a candy-striped blouse by Bellville Sassoon. ABOVE, This printed silk suit by Donald Campbell was worn several times in 1982.

looked her most beautiful. For just that day," said Emanuel, "things seemed to be right."

Within months of her engagement, Diana had already begun to develop a stronger sense of which kinds of clothes worked and which didn't on her newly willowy frame. The softly tailored clothes by Bill Pashley, Donald Campbell and Bellville Sassoon (her first favorite designer label) worn during her honeymoon beautifully showcased her youthful appeal. At the same time, her unique ability to understand the power of clothes and the messages they can convey was already becoming apparent. As Diana became more fluent in her fashion vocabulary, she was more inclined to trust her own judgment rather than rely solely on the suggestions of her advisors. When a tour of Wales was planned for the end of October, Diana selected just the right clothes for the occasion: a suit by Donald Campbell in the Welsh national colors—red and dark green. "I received a call from Anna Harvey and she said one must have an entire green leg and shoes," said Campbell. "I thought from a fashion point of view I could quite see that, and we'll get Manolo [Blahnik] round to do the shoes. I do know on the actual day, Diana wore red shoes and white tights. This was a non-fashion thing to do but it was something I suppose she wanted to do. I think Diana had an instinct from the very early days about what people expected from her and I think she was quite a chameleon—she changed according to circumstances. That's the essence of her, really. Instinctively she may have felt that she didn't want to be a killer fashion plate. When she was meeting the folks back in Wales, people were more apt to notice a pair of red shoes."

With the wedding and honeymoon behind her, Diana continued to search out designers to create the vast wardrobe she now needed for her role as Princess of Wales. While other women her own age were free to experiment with the latest styles, Diana's choices were governed by protocol.

Although she may have tried at first to blend in with the other royals, it was impossible for Diana to do so. Her luminous beauty made her an ideal cover girl.

Bright colors were the preferred choice, hats must always be worn for official engagements and skirts must never be too short. There had to be an appropriate outfit for every occasion. She was now on display every time she was seen in public, and every detail of what she wore was scrutinized in the press. Many of the fashion editors who had heralded Diana as an elegant young woman when she first appeared on the pages of London's newspapers, were now making stinging criticisms. (The infamous Mr. Blackwell awarded Diana the dubious distinction of being one of the Ten Worst Dressed Women in 1982.) The general consensus was that she could look as dazzling in the most casual of styles as she did in elegant eveningwear, but those clothes that fell somewhere in the middle were often where she made her biggest fashion mistakes. And while she frequently dressed too old for her age, her admirers felt that Diana usually looked all the more charming and endearing as a result. The Princess was wisely not attempting to win over the elitist fashion crowd. Instead, she seemed to spend a great deal of time and effort attempting to please the throngs of people that waited for hours behind barricades in hopes of catching a fleeting glimpse of Britain's newest star. They found no fault with her seesawing efforts to look stylish—she consistently garnered rave reviews from her adoring public.

Diana came to understand there was a huge difference between what she could wear in her private and public lives. "She did have two definite wardrobes," said Sassoon. "A function wardrobe and then a private wardrobe. She couldn't wear jersey dresses publicly at that time. Mind you, she was the first to do a lot of things—like wearing trousers and tuxedo jackets to formal engagements." After she married, Diana made dramatic changes to both wardrobes. Her personal style had previously been defined primarily by an assortment of casual clothes: whimsical sweaters and straight-legged jeans from Harvey Nichols and silk and cotton floral patterned dresses and skirts from Harrods. All that changed overnight. Shopping, once one of her favorite pastimes, had now become an overwhelming job. With virtually no guidance except her own judgment and the discrete enthusiasm of the designers she patronized, she found herself spending a great deal of time looking for the right clothes. "In the beginning she found it quite difficult to know what kind of clothes were required and she tended to follow what the other royals did," said Sassoon.

Although she may have tried at first to blend in with the other royals, it was impossible for Diana to do so. The Palace had reassured the Princess that after the wedding the rabid attention of the press would subside. Nothing could have been further from the truth. Diana's luminous, photogenic beauty made her an ideal cover girl. But in 1982, as the world was in the throes of its fervent love affair with Diana, the Princess

Diana helped popularize a more feminine style in maternity clothes. Bellville Sassoon designed one of her favorite dresses, this empire-waisted gown in white silk, which Diana wore to meet Elizabeth Taylor in March of 1982.

ABOVE, Diana wore flowing dresses in pale colors during much of her first pregnancy. OPPOSITE, In November of 1982, only a few months after the birth of Prince William, she appeared at a gala in this one-shoulder dress, by Bruce Oldfield looking alarmingly thin.

was suffering through a difficult pregnancy and extreme feelings of depression. Troubles were beginning to plague her marriage. While Diana may have felt confused and unhappy, she showed no outwards signs of such conflict. In front of the ever-present cameras that now documented her every move, she actually appeared more confident and beautiful than ever before. From this point on, it is difficult, if not impossible, to recall a single photograph where she didn't appear radiant. "She glowed in front of the camera," said one royal watcher. "It was as if she developed this sheen and she could give some of her lonely self to the camera."

During her pregnancy with Prince William, Diana made few public appearances. When she did, she managed to touch off a whole new series of fashion trends. Her maternity wardrobe was full of frilly feminine styles from Bellville Sassoon and Catherine Walker. Diana seemed eager to dress the part of expectant mother. She usually opted for clothes in eye-catching colors for daytime dressing–like the voluminous multi-colored wool coat by Bellville Sassoon worn for the announcement of her pregnancy in November of 1981. Her evening clothes were frequently empire-waisted with lots of frills and lace. "She loved large, romantic kinds of dandy-type collars," said Sassoon, who would send sketches to Diana and receive them back with notes from her outlining the kinds of details she wanted to incorporate into the designs. (Those styles she was most enthusiastic about would be marked with 'Please!' at the top of the illustration.) "She wanted something framing her neck that would distract from the fact that she was big," he said. What she had previously done in popularizing frilly blouses and multi-strand pearl chokers (the first true Diana emblem copied around the world), she was now doing for feminine-looking maternity clothes.

In November of 1982, just a few months after Prince William was born, Diana appeared at a fashion show in a thirties-style, one-shoulder ruffled dress by Bruce Oldfield that caused the crowd to gasp. But it was not out of admiration for Diana's innovative wardrobe choice. The dress accentuated Diana's alarmingly thin shoulders and arms and seemed to lend credence to the rumors that she was suffering from an eating disorder. Diana recalled those troubling days and her battle with bulimia that began on her honeymoon in her 1995 interview with the BBC's Martin Bashir: "You'd wake up in the morning feeling you didn't want to get out of bed, you felt misunderstood and just very, very low on yourself. . .I received a great deal of treatment, but I knew myself that actually what I needed was space and time to adapt to all the different roles that had come my way. In the space of a year, my whole life had changed, turned upside down. It had its wonderful moments but it also had its challenging moments and I could see where the rough edges needed to be smoothed." Diana was intent on becoming more poised and polished in her role as Princess of Wales and she realized refining her wardrobe was an important part of the process. Now thinner than ever before, she began experimenting with sleeker styles for both day and evening. She wore clothes from a host of different designers, including Jasper Conran, Gina Fratini, Caroline Charles (who designed the charming tartan dress Diana wore to the Braemar Games in Scotland) and Jan Vanvelden. Publicly Diana appeared more confident in her newly fashionable clothes, but privately her battle with bulimia worsened and would continue to plague her for years.

When she became pregnant with Prince Harry in 1984, she was not in any rush to get back into maternity clothes. By this time, Diana was looking for ways to assert and express herself in an increasingly stifling environment. The loose-fitting coats and dresses from her first pregnancy had been replaced by more tailored contemporary styles in monochromatic colors (red was a favorite). Her eveningwear was more dramatic than ever before and was frequently embellished with gold or silver (Diana loved silver accessories

Diana was wisely not attempting to win over the elitist fashion crowd. Instead, she spent a great deal of effort trying to please the public. They found no fault with her seesawing efforts to look stylish.

and often wore metallic shoes and purses).

"What's interesting for me having dressed her before she got married is to see the change in her afterwards," said Sassoon. "Dealing with royalty is such a formal thing. Before she was married it was always, 'Please call me Diana.' But after she got married, it was very much the Princess of Wales—in a gentle way. But you had to appreciate she was a royal princess." Sassoon remembers her as an ideal client who always sent thank-you notes after she wore one of his designs. "I think that until she had her second child, she wasn't really quite so into fashion. She was a joy to dress. She didn't like a lot of fittings—she liked to choose something and have one fitting and that was it. She never took fashion really seriously. She would never say, 'Oh, I don't like this or that.' She had a great sense of humor about it all and didn't make a fuss. I do dress most of the royals, who make much more of a fuss about occasions and about royal dressing. There is a lot of politics in dressing so many members of the royal family. It's tricky. There were certain members of the royal family who wanted to wear the same things as her and she didn't actually like it. One particular member was great for going to Catherine Walker, myself and one or two other designers and wanting the same dress—which wasn't greatly appreciated."

By the time Diana reached her 22nd birthday, she had shed her image as "Shy Lady Di—fashion neophyte" and had moved on to the next stage of her public life. While she had yet to find her style (it seemed to depend largely on what designer she was wearing), she was beginning to gamble more with her look and seemed eager to experiment. Diana had also begun to understand and work with many aspects of royal dressing that she had never dealt with before. "The thing about the royals is that they do have the most amazing jewels," said Sassoon. "So it often happens that you have to design a dress around a piece of jewelry." The young woman who just a few years ago owned little more than a few pairs of hoop earrings, a man's watch and a gold letter "D" pendant was well on her way to amassing one of the most impressive jewelry collections in the world. And while Diana was struggling to find the right look in her clothing, she carried off her jewelry with a naturalness and grace, choosing eveningwear that served as an elegant backdrop for her most striking pieces.

The sweet, unpretentious young girl who had married her prince was embarking on what would be a series of dramatic transformations. Diana was a woman whose public role had fostered, at least outwardly, a newfound sense of maturity. "Shy Di" was evolving into "Sly Di." She was beginning to reshape the role of a modern princess for the mass-media age and her look became her most powerful tool in doing so. "Before she found her voice," said Donald Campbell, "literally and figuratively—she communicated to the world through her clothes." A fashion star was born.

Diana quickly adopted the practice of offsetting her jewelry collection with simple, streamlined evening dresses. This pink chiffon gown by Victor Edelstein is accessorized with the Spencer family tiara and a sapphire and diamond necklace with matching earrings. The brooch is a hand-painted miniature of the Queen surrounded by diamonds, set in platinum and topped by a tiny Tudor crown.

2

THE AMBASSADOR OF BRITISH FASHION

The moment Diana became Princess of Wales she was unofficially awarded another title: Ambassador of British Fashion. While it was widely believed the Princess was required to wear clothing from British designers, it was, in fact, her choice to do so. Elizabeth and David Emanuel, Bruce Oldfield, Catherine Walker, Bellville Sassoon and Victor Edelstein quickly became part of her fashion lexicon. She single-handedly revived Britain's millinery industry by donning the designs of Philip Somerville, Graham Smith and Marina Killery. While Diana had amassed one of the most stunning collections of jewels in the world, her penchant for "paste" helped popularize costume jewelry worldwide. "She put British design on the map and brought it center stage," said Elizabeth Emanuel. Her incandescent beauty, status and incredible charisma made her one of fashion's brightest stars. Diana became Britain's reigning Queen of Style—and the best walking advertisement the fashion industry had ever had.

While it was widely believed Diana was required to wear clothing from British designers, it was, in fact, her choice to do so.

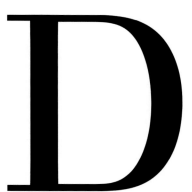

Diana had learned from the very beginning of her public life that appearances counted for a great deal. She videotaped every one of her television appearances, carefully scrutinizing each detail, including her hair and makeup and, of course, her clothing. This was done not out of vanity but rather to execute her "job" as best she could. "I think she was very much aware that people expected her to dress up," remembers Emanuel. "She didn't want to disappoint them." And she rarely did. Shortly after the birth of her two sons, Diana was back in the spotlight looking more elegant and beautiful than ever before. Although privately she continued to battle bulimia and a deep depression spurred on by her husband's infidelities, publicly she maintained her game face by taking refuge in her increasingly fashionable wardrobe. Diana was just beginning to recognize the power of her image. No royal before her had ever taken such a strong interest in fashion or understood so well how it could be used to help communicate with the public. By 1985, Diana's role as the ambassador of British fashion had made her a budding style icon to women around the world.

In March of that year, Diana was the guest of honor at a reception held at London's Lancaster House to kick-off the beginning of Fashion Week. She turned to Bellville Sassoon for something suitably chic for the occasion. David Sassoon recalls that the Princess chose an unusual dressing gown-and-trouser look—with somewhat mixed results. "The style was very fashionable at the time," said the designer. "It was a look that had been popularized by Ralph Lauren that was elegant and sophisticated, so I was pleased when she chose to wear it. When I saw her at the event, I realized she had worn the gown without the trousers. It was certainly not the way I had envisioned her wearing it, but she had done her own thing."

During her many public appearances in 1985, Diana seemed intent on experimenting with several different looks. Like many women during that time, the Princess favored large

square shoulders in her day dresses and suits, like those that were ever-present on the soap operas she loved to watch. "Dynasty Di," a moniker culled from the highly-rated eighties television series, was a label that the Princess was given when she began emulating the "power dressing" look. For a trip to Italy, the Emanuels took that look to the extreme when they designed for Diana a long green plaid wool coat with a squared-off collar and oversized hat. The press criticized the ensemble, calling it "overpowering." The Princess, who considered the couple's designs "dramatic," loved it, and her legion of fans agreed. "She was very keen on the color and was very game to wear the hat," said Emanuel. Once again, Diana had shown that while her choices were not always considered to be the height of fashion, she instinctively knew how people wanted to view her. Knowing she had succeeded gave her tremendous satisfaction.

While Diana's wardrobe had become the subject of many stories, its cost was also coming under scrutiny. The Princess once complained to a friend that she was criticized both for wearing too many new outfits, and for repeatedly wearing

PAGE 49, On royal tours Diana often showcased British fashion with "theme" outfits like this one worn in Tokyo in 1990. Philip Somerville's pillbox hat featured a rising sun, the national symbol of Japan. The suit is by Catherine Walker. ABOVE, Diana liked the "dramatic" designs of Elizabeth and David Emanuel. In 1985, she wore their emerald-green plaid coat and matching hat during a trip to Italy.

Diana chose another Emanuel dress for a 1985 trip to Australia. This one-shoulder aquamarine design in silk organza was a favorite. Diana added her own style by substituting her Queen Mary choker for her tiara, which had accidentally been left behind.

the same outfit. One particular floral dress by Bellville Sassoon was a favorite; Diana wore it frequently over a period of five years. "There was actually an article written about it saying the Princess should throw it out because she wore it so much," said David Sassoon. "She called it her 'working dress' that she liked for hospital visits. She told me children apparently love color and she thought if she wore a bright-colored dress, they'd have a memory of her visit. So she always seemed to wear it around children."

Before her trip to Italy, there was speculation that Diana had spent an extravagant £80,000 on a wardrobe for the occasion. While she did buy several new outfits, this figure is considered to be a wild exaggeration. As a royal, Diana was expected to dress the part and that involved a great deal of organization. Every detail was meticulously cataloged so that she always knew when and where she last wore an outfit. Two dressers (one always accompanied her on her royal tours) carefully maintained a wardrobe that by the mid-eighties contained more than eighty suits, nearly 150 gowns, over seventy hats and 100 pairs of earrings. Each outfit was hung on padded hangers and stored in one of Diana's huge walk-in closets in garment bags from Eximious, one of the companies that holds a Royal Warrant for supplying products or services to the royal household.

Designer Tomasz Starzewski, who first met Diana at Earl Spencer's wedding in 1989 and then began dressing her, explained how the Princess carefully considered the price of each outfit when planning her wardrobe. "All the designers who continually supplied her had a certain budget," he said. "Catherine [Walker] had the highest budget and Victor [Edelstein], who dressed her for a certain period and was the only real couturier who dressed

Emerald green ballgown
worn by HRH The Princess of Wales
on her trip to Australia.
Designed by
Elizabeth + David Emanuel

Emanuel

her, was the most expensive. So he was always careful. We all knew if we went over a certain price she would not buy it." Everything, said Starzewski, was always bought and paid for. "As British designers, we were not allowed to give her clothes because of the whole system of royal warrants. You actually had to bill Buckingham Palace and were paid by Prince Charles. Any gifts would have been perceived as bribery and influence."

When Diana went on a royal tour representing the monarchy, the cost of her official wardrobe was paid out of a special fund. Bills from designers and various shops were signed by Diana's lady-in-waiting, Anne Beckwith-Smith, and forwarded to the Wales office in St. James Palace. (Some bills were also paid with an American Express card that bore the name "Duchy of Cornwall.") But while Diana did love clothes and shopped a great deal, she was not a spend-thrift. She often tried to economize by asking designers to re-style her clothes by changing a hemline or retooling a jacket. The clothes she no longer wore were often lent or given to her sisters.

During her trip to Australia later that year, one of the most striking dresses Diana wore was one that had made a previous appearance two years earlier. The frothy aquamarine organza and silk dress with crystal beading, by the Emanuels, shimmered on Diana as she swirled across the dance floor with Charles at the Southern Cross Hotel in Melbourne. The dress, with its dropped waist and one-shoulder detailing, was made even more memorable by Diana's choice of accessories. After she had discovered she had forgotten her tiara, she improvised at the last minute and wore her Queen Mary choker as a headband. The look was quintessential Diana, circa 1985.

Diana opted for a more serious "working wardrobe" for her first trip to Washington, D. C. in 1985. During her "power dressing" phase in the mid-eighties, she wore many designs by Bruce Oldfield, including a royal blue and black jersey dress, OPPOSITE, and ABOVE, an ivory suit.

Bruce Oldfield was largely responsible for Diana's most glamorous looks worn during the early to mid-eighties. He was one of the many designers introduced to her by *Vogue's* Anna Harvey. "We were told to make an English size 10, an American size 8 and a slightly longer skirt and slightly longer sleeves—and that was it," remembered the designer. "We first met her after the wedding at the end of August 1981 when she actually came to my showroom." Diana's presence caused quite a commotion. "We didn't know how to handle it and handle her," said Oldfield. "But she was very, very easy. She put everybody at ease. She didn't like formality, so it was nice all around. Everybody got on well. She got on with my partner and the fitters and so it was good. It was a very good start."

Diana became a regular visitor to Oldfield's shop on Beauchamp Place, where she would "rummage through the table looking at fabrics." Contrary to popular belief, the Princess did not have most of her clothes made especially for her. "To a great extent, she usually chose things from my collection. She had some things customized, especially when there was a special tour to some place like the Middle East where there were certain dress codes. Then, even more restrictions were put on her," noted Oldfield. Those restrictions included making sure there wasn't too much of the royal figure—however fabulous it had become—on display. "It was quite difficult for her as a young woman whose style had not yet emerged and who had to take on board all of the restrictions of royal dressing. She was very much a slave to what was expected of her. She would buy things that were suitable for specific occasions. Skirts couldn't be more than two inches above the knee. We would have liked them to have been four inches above the knee but in no way was

Diana dazzled a star-studded crowd at a White House State Dinner in 1985 as she danced with John Travolta wearing one of her most famous dresses—a draped navy blue velvet gown by Victor Edelstein.

While Diana's clothes generated a great deal of attention, it was her hair that sparked a new trend every time she experimented with a different look.

that allowed in the mid-eighties. Every time she put her legs out of the limousine there was a camera trying to get a shot. It was difficult, but she took it all in stride. It became a bit of a game. You know, 'How can I get out of a car without showing ten inches of leg?'"

But Diana did opt to wear some of Oldfield's flashiest designs—the famous one-shoulder ruffled dress and the open-back, silver lamé gown among them. "It was quite often that we were asked to make things a bit more showy than we normally did because she had to stand out. Of course later on, she didn't need showy frocks to stand out. In fact, I don't even think she did at the beginning." The glittering silver design was worn several times and always sparked a firestorm of media attention. "It was very daring for its day," said Oldfield. "She was becoming more comfortable with herself, right about the mid-eighties when she got the label "Dynasty Di." She liked sexy clothes. She wore the lamé dress in 1985 when she was my date for Dr. Barnardo's (the orphanage where Oldfield grew up), and there were other guests there that night, including Joan Collins. Diana (who was Barnardo's honorary

president) was at her most glamorous—she looked like a movie star." It was her unique star power that drew so many people to the dinner, said Oldfield. "We were charging £100 a head—that was an enormous amount of money at the time," recalled the designer. "Then, three years later we sold 1200 seats at £250 a ticket. It was the Princess of Wales' pulling power. It was quite extraordinary. The other thing that was quite funny was when we got up to dance, she said the thing that amazed her most was how whenever she danced anywhere you would think people would crush in on her. I asked her, 'Don't you get frightened?' and she said, 'I don't get frightened because there's always this sort of magic yard or, you know, two feet of space around me, because people actually don't get close to you, they stay away.'"

Oldfield used to jokingly scold Diana whenever he spotted her standing a certain way that was unflattering to her or her clothes. "She had this habit of pushing her knees back and locking them. She'd have her legs slightly apart and sort of put her hands behind her back and push her legs back. It would wreck havoc with straight

In this early undated head shot, Diana displayed the qualities that helped make her the most photographed woman in the world.

Diana's hairstyles frequently made headlines: TOP, In 1984, going blonder and longer after Prince Harry's birth. CENTER, the "Teddy Boy" style. Women all over the world were eager to emulate the 1986 cut. BOTTOM, Diana's hairstyle by Sam McKnight gave her a chic new look in 1990. OPPOSITE, By 1993, Diana's short, layered cut had become her signature.

LEFT, During a 1986 trip to the Gulf, Diana wore glittering crescent moon earrings that were believed to be a gift from her host. In fact, they were from her own collection of costume jewelry. BELOW, She received a diamond necklace and earring set from the Sultan of Oman, which she wore for the first time with the Spencer family tiara in Germany in November of 1987. OPPOSITE, She adorned a flamenco-inspired dress by Murray Arbeid with Butler & Wilson's star-shaped enamel and diamanté medal for a 1986 film premiere.

skirts," he recalled. "I'd often think, 'What on earth have you done with that skirt? It fit you fine.' The other thing that I always used to tell her about was stooping. She was quite tall and that's why she always wore these little two-inch heels."

When Diana and Charles visited Washington, D. C. together for the first time in November of 1985, *Vogue* reported that the Princess swept into the capitol city with luggage that weighed in at seven thousand pounds. Diana had accurately assessed that she should leave her more frilly fashions at home and opted to dress for all her public appearances in more streamlined clothes. Her 'working wardrobe' of well-cut suits and sleekly tailored dresses (many from Oldfield's collection) looked suitably chic—and serious—during the day. It was on this trip at a State Dinner at the White House that one of the most striking evening gowns ever worn by Diana was seen for the first time. In the "John Travolta dress," a stunning column of navy blue velvet by Victor Edelstein, Diana was at her most glamorous and beautiful. Another Diana emblem was also unveiled that evening: an enormous sapphire brooch surrounded by diamonds (given to her by the Queen Mother) set on a pearl choker. The Princess was not a great fan of brooches and when she pinned it on the dress, it looked and felt too heavy. When it was suggested she convert it into a necklace—Garrard refashioned the piece—Diana was thrilled with the result. She did not need her tiara that night. In her most sophisticated gown to date, accessorized with the glittering necklace, she reigned over the crowd as the most beautiful—and best dressed—woman in the room.

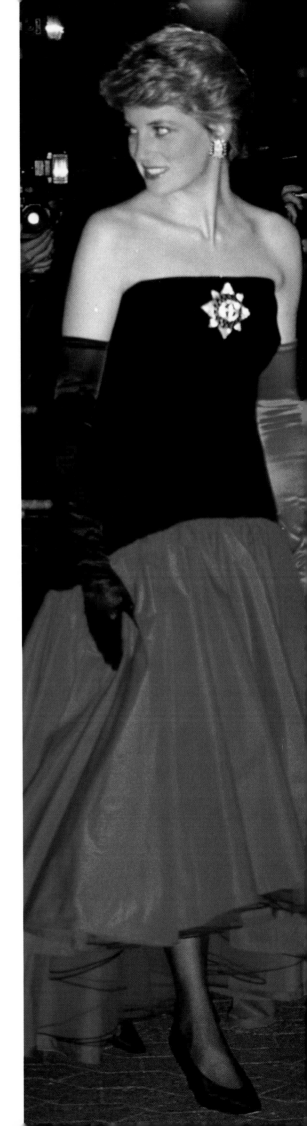

Diana adopted a tentative style that often vacillated, depending on whose clothes she wore.

Diana's transformation from Sloane Ranger to the world's number-one cover girl didn't happen by chance. She relied heavily on the expertise of people like *Vogue's* Anna Harvey (who, except for her own tribute to her friend in the October 1997 issue of British *Vogue,* has remained silent about her relationship with Diana) and other close confidantes whose judgment she trusted. Hairstylist Richard Dalton first met Diana while working at Head Lines, a South Kensington salon that both she and her mother frequented when Diana was just eighteen years old. At the time, Kevin Shanley was cutting her hair and was later responsible for the first "Lady Di" style with its layers and heavy fringe. Dalton occasionally filled in for Shanley and took over for him in 1984.

The Scottish-born stylist was Diana's hairdresser for ten years, acting as both a beauty and fashion consultant. "She would start the day early," said Dalton, who frequently styled Diana's hair twice a day. "I was always with her around 7:30 or 8:00. I had a regular job as well, but she would have to have her hair done first thing in the morning. I would go in and she'd say, 'What should I wear today?' There would be three outfits hanging up and I would ask, 'Where are you going?' and she would tell me, we'd choose and I'd do her hair. Sometimes we'd talk, sometimes we wouldn't. Sometimes she'd say, 'You've got fifteen minutes,' and the sparks would fly from the brush."

While Diana's clothes generated a great deal of attention, in the mid-eighties it was her hair that sparked a new trend every time she experimented with a different look. "She always wondered why people were so interested in her hair," said Dalton. " She used to say to me people would tell her, 'You look like you just had your hair done.' She'd say, 'They don't really know I just have.' She felt she was in a fortunate position to have all trappings, like someone to do her hair."

Dalton remembered when Diana made headlines by wearing her newly long hair in a chignon for the State Opening of Parliament in 1984. "It knocked the Queen off the front page," he recalled. The story stayed in the papers for

This long, pleated dinner dress with its beaded neck and waist by Japanese designer Yuki was first worn to a banquet in Tokyo in 1986. It typified Diana's glitzy "Dynasty" style.

days afterwards when the Princess wore her hair tucked back in combs the following day. Realizing that the publicity surrounding every aspect of her look could avert attention from the rest of the royals, Diana and Dalton were careful to make subsequent changes in a more subtle way. "We were all majorly bowled over by the attention. After that we became cautious because her hair was such a major thing. If we were going to change her style, like when we were going to Saudi Arabia where we decided her hair would probably be more suitable short, we'd do it over a period of weeks, so it would be every other day, snip, snip, snip, so you didn't notice it. But if you looked over a period of a month, there was a major change."

Dalton, who also accompanied Diana on royal tours abroad, remembered her as a woman who possessed both a playful sense of humor and meticulous organizational skills. "We were in Venice and she and the Prince were going down the Grand Canal on the royal barge when she saw a can of hair spray floating nearby. She said to the Prince, 'I think Richard has fallen in.' But then when they turned the corner they saw me up at the top window and we all laughed. There were lots and lots of funny, funny things that went on. We had great times." Dalton said Diana was also a woman who took her responsibilities quite seriously. When it came to preparing for a state visit or other special events, no detail was too big or too small. "She was completely professional in everything she did," he said. "She would study the rundown on the people she was going to meet and she would know a lot about them.

She was given a job to do and did it one hundred percent. She was always very gracious about everything and always wrote me letters and thanked me for being patient and running around trying to find gloves or a piece of jewelry or something."

Although Diana had one of the most impressive jewelry collections in the world (some estimates put its value at over $27 million), her tastes were decidedly eclectic. Some of her most priceless jewels were given to her as gifts by various members of the royal family, including the Queen Mary tiara, an emerald and diamond choker and the newly fashioned sapphire and pearl choker. During their marriage, Prince Charles also had many pieces of jewelry designed especially for Diana: a gold and pearl heart-shaped necklace, an antique emerald and diamond bracelet and a gold charm bracelet to which he made regular additions. One item that caught the Prince's eye was a diamond Prince of Wales brooch that belonged to the late Duchess of Windsor. It was set to be auctioned in Switzerland in 1987. The dazzling piece ultimately went to Elizabeth Taylor, who made a successful bid.

"She always loved jewelry, particularly earrings," said David Thomas, the Crown Jeweller. "Sapphires and pearls were particular favorites." Diana received a suite of sapphire and diamond jewelry which included earrings, necklaces and bracelets as a wedding gift from the Saudi Royal Family. But as she often did with her jewelry, she

PINK/WHITE
DOGTOOTH CHECK
FABRIC HAT
[GRO]TGRSHAM BOW AT
BACK.
[P]INK EYE VEIL.

Milliner Philip Somerville
collaborated with designer
Catherine Walker to
create this hat worn with a
matching coatdress to a
Thanksgiving service
in 1990.

Philip Somerville created a red boater with a black snood to accompany a Rifat Ozbek suit Diana wore to France in 1987. "You're going to France, so you've got to have something that's interesting," Somerville told the Princess.

added her own unique style. She converted the bracelet into a choker and wore it on a ribbon around her neck.

Many of Diana's favorite pieces came from a surprisingly unconventional source–the popular shop Butler & Wilson which was well known for its extensive collections of costume jewelry. Diana, who frequently visited their Fulham Road boutique, was as comfortable in faux diamonds and pearls as she was in the priceless royal family heirlooms. "She would come in and buy loads and loads of earrings and pearls," says Simon Wilson. The first item she ever bought at the store, silver bow-and-heart drop earrings for which she paid £20, became an overnight best-seller when Diana was photographed wearing them at several official occasions. The Princess also wore many other Butler & Wilson "paste" pieces including gold button earrings, a diamanté and black glass serpent brooch, a bejeweled medieval cross and a star-shaped enamel and diamanté medal that she pinned to the front of a strapless

HRH PRINCESS OF WALES.

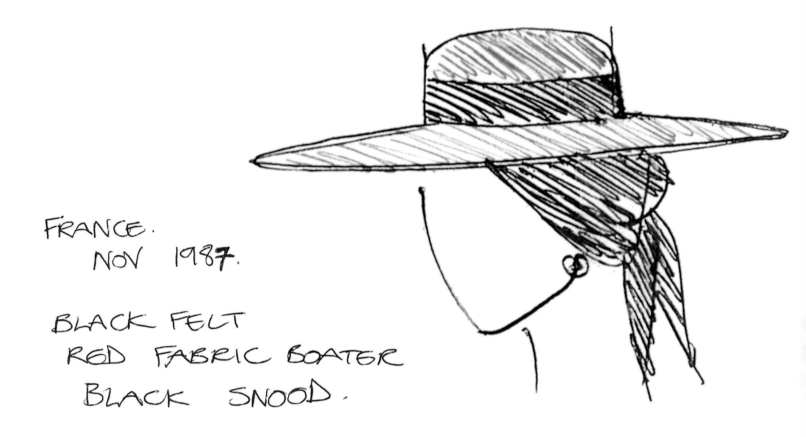

FRANCE.
NOV 1987.

BLACK FELT
RED FABRIC BOATER
BLACK SNOOD.

Murray Arbeid gown.

One of the most famous Butler & Wilson styles ever worn by Diana was the crescent moon diamanté earrings seen during a 1986 trip to the Persian Gulf. The whimsical earrings in the shape of Saudi Arabia's national symbol were widely reported to have been an extravagant present from her hosts. In fact, Diana had bought them the day before her trip for just £23 at her favorite costume jewelry shop. Diana did receive a gift from the Sultan of Oman during the tour: a crescent-shaped diamond and sapphire necklace and earring set that she first wore on a trip to Germany in 1987. But just as frequently she could be spotted wearing pieces that any other fashionable woman in London could afford. "She was a young girl," said Wilson. "When she had to go out wearing the real thing she would, but she also liked to buy things just because she liked them."

In those early years, Diana adopted a tentative style that often vacillated depending on whose clothes she wore. There was no instruction manual on how to look or act like a royal, and if one did exist, its rules would certainly not have been meant for Diana. The frumpy fashion favored by her relatives didn't suit her youthful style, but she did have to follow protocol, which meant incorporating hats and gloves into her wardrobe. While she quickly dispensed with gloves except on the most formal occasions (Diana hated them and preferred hand-to-hand contact), she learned—with a great deal of trial and error—how to wear hats without looking dowdy. Before becoming Princess of Wales, she had only worn hats to a few engagements, like a friend's wedding. Now, every outfit for an official occasion or state tour needed a hat. By the end of 1986, she owned 75 of them.

BLUE SILK TURBAN
WHITE STRAW BRIM
TWO BLUE QUILLS.

"They raved about her and said it was a fabulous look that nobody had seen on her before. We had thought of it to cover up her hair."

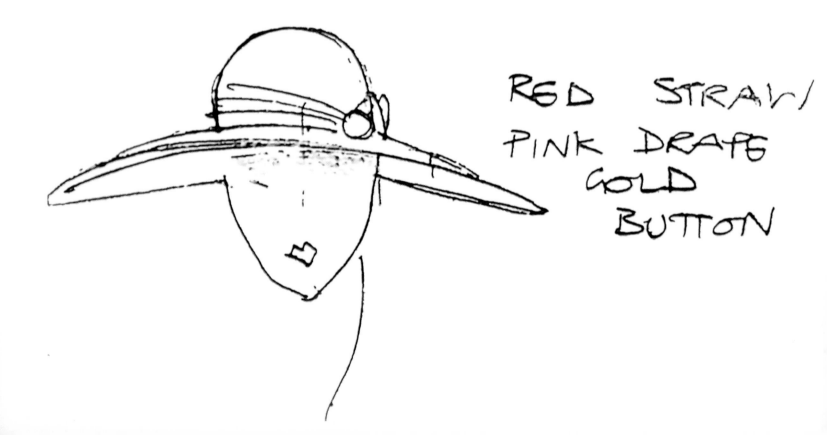

RED STRAW/
PINK DRAPE
GOLD
BUTTON

In 1989, Diana wore several of Somerville's most memorable designs for her trip to Abu Dhabi. LEFT, A blue and white turban honored the country's custom which calls for women to cover their heads. BELOW, A pink and red wide-brimmed hat was designed at Diana's suggestion to be worn with a silk Catherine Walker coatdress.

After making some of her biggest fashion mistakes with smallish, matronly hats from John Boyd (who had been her mother's milliner), Diana moved on to more modern, flattering designs, and is largely credited with having made hats chic again for young women. Most of the styles she wore from 1986 until the end of her life were from Philip Somerville, who also designs for the Queen and other members of the royal family. Somerville was introduced to Diana by Richard Dalton, who had been asked by the Princess to track down the designer of a hat she saw on television. "We got a call asking if I could see the Princess if she came to the shop," said Somerville. "Of course, I said yes. When she arrived, she was standing there with Richard, and of course there were cars parked outside and security. The very first time I met the Princess I was struck by her physical being and the way she held herself–there aren't too many people that have that quality."

Diana quickly developed a strong rapport with Somerville and entrusted him with making her hats for virtually every official engagement. "She had a rather large head. That meant trying on a lot of hats. We used to have a lot of laughs over the fact that the samples sat on the top of her head. They never looked right until we'd had a fitting, so we had to visualize a lot from that first day in the shop. So after that, of course, I made the shapes to take to the Palace in her size. In the end, we had a wooden block which was made to the exact size of the Princess's

"TEMPLE"
SILK CROWN
STRAW BRIM.

Somerville's "Temple" hat was worn with a silk crepe de chine dress by Catherine Walker on a 1989 trip to Hong Kong. Diana worked closely with the designers, noting which accessories she planned to wear on the designers' sketches.

"She used to tell me that her hats were always noticed. Afterwards, we'd change the crown so she could wear it again."

head." Diana made regular appointments with Somerville for many years. "Whenever she went on a royal tour, she needed hats," he said. "But she would never wear hats to a hospital because she said you couldn't cuddle a child with a hat on." The designer was a frequent visitor at Kensington Palace, where he sometimes conferred with Prince Charles on his wife's fashion choices. "I remember once we were there and she called out to her husband, the Prince, 'Darling, come and see the lovely hats that Mr. Somerville has made for me.' She said, 'Aren't these big hats wonderful?' And he said, 'Yes, very lovely. I do like my wife in smaller hats as well,' and I said, 'Yes, you are right, I quite agree. Your wife can wear big and small hats.'"

Although Diana was not a huge fan of hats (and wore them infrequently after her divorce), she looked stunning in the right shapes. She had quickly learned how they could add impact to her look. Somerville worked closely with Diana's favorite designer, Catherine Walker, to ensure her hats coordinated perfectly with her many outfits. "I'd get a call from the Palace saying the Princess had two or three outfits she wanted hats

for. So I'd do something like six or eight different shapes that I thought suited her. Sometimes Catherine would have the outfits sent here and I could look at them or send sketches. That made it easier to visualize." To make sure the hats were an exact match to Walker's dresses or suits, Somerville used fabric provided by the designer.

In the beginning, Diana preferred subtle shapes and colors. "She loved veils," said Somerville. "They added an air of mystery, and of course in the early days she was very, very shy. She could hide behind them." But as Diana grew more confident, her choices grew bolder and more daring. In 1987, she was planning to accompany Charles on a trip to France and approached Somerville for some wardrobe advice. "She said, 'What on earth am I going to wear? My hair won't be good.' She was flying in and going straight to an appointment and she was a bit worried because she wouldn't have much time to change on such a short flight," recalled the designer. "I said, 'Well, you're going to France, so you've got to have something that's interesting because France is so fashionable.'" Somerville suggested a red boater with a black

HALO.
PINK
STRAW
PURPLE PETERSHAM.

snood to wear with a red Rifat Ozbek suit, and Diana was enthusiastic about the idea. "When she arrived in Paris, they raved about her and said it was a fabulous look that nobody had seen on her before. Of course, we had thought of it to cover up her hair." Somerville often offered guidance when Diana asked how she could complete a look. "Another time she'd say, 'What about earrings?' and I'd say, 'Why don't you try and get two more buttons from Catherine and have earrings made?' and she said, 'Oh, yes, that's a good idea.' She had that done a few times."

In 1989, Diana wore three of Somerville's most memorable designs. One of her favorite hats was actually a collaborative effort between the designer and the Princess created to complement a striking pink and red coatdress by Catherine Walker. "Diana showed me a sketch of the outfit," recalled Somerville, "and I said, 'Gosh, pink and red? And she said, 'Isn't it marvelous? It's my idea.' I said, 'What a pity. I never thought about pink and red.' And in the end it was quite terrific and so I was wrong. It did work. I think it was a very nice look, actually–very interesting."

For Diana's arrival in Abu Dhabi in March of 1989, Somerville faced the challenge of designing

PINK STRAW
PINK
DRAPE

Diana's most successful hat styles came from Philip Somerville. His eye-catching shapes included both unusual and classic designs, like the "halo" worn to Ascot in 1990, ABOVE, and the oversized cloche OPPOSITE, BOTTOM, hat which she favored for trips to sunnier climates.

Polka dots adorned everything from accessories to sportswear during the mid-eighties, and had long been a favorite Diana look. LEFT, This Victor Edelstein dress was originally designed with a peplum in 1986, but appeared newly sleek at Ascot in 1988. BELOW, Diana's spotted skirt with matching anklets from Mondi worn to a 1986 polo match were far from cutting edge, but London boutiques were overwhelmed with requests for similar styles. OPPOSITE, Diana's "majorette" suit by Catherine Walker, worn with a hat by Graham Smith for Kangol, clearly showed that she didn't take fashion too seriously at the time.

something stylish yet appropriate for a country where custom called for the Princess's head to be covered. The milliner presented Diana with the idea of wearing a turban to coordinate with a white and royal blue suit by Catherine Walker. She jumped at the chance to wear something so dramatic. "At the time Catherine's clothes had a very classic look," said Somerville. "And I thought, we've got to really make something different. I went over and said, 'I wonder if you'd wear a turban?' and she said, 'I'd love to, let me try one on.' So we put the turban on and I was worried about submerging all of her hair. She was very conscious of her hair and that it flattered and softened her face. She did have some concerns about her neck—everybody has features they're not fond of." When Diana tried the turban on, both designer and client liked it, but Somerville felt something was missing. "I took two or three brims and put a little cuff on because sometimes we juggle crowns and brims together. I put the brim over the hat and she thought it was marvelous."

Somerville's famous hat in the shape of a Chinese temple was worn in Hong Kong with a red and purple silk Catherine Walker dress in November of that year (and seen again at Ascot in 1990). It was one of several "theme" hats he designed as an homage to various countries Diana visited. "When she was going to Turkey we would do something with a Turkish look, for Japan we did a hat with the rising sun on the side, which the Emperor found quite amusing, and for Bangkok I got the idea of doing a temple," said Somerville. "It was quite successful and she used to tell me when she got back from the tours that the hats were always noticed. Afterwards, we changed the crown so she could wear it again. You could do those kinds of details on hats, you couldn't do it with dresses very much."

Somerville worked with Diana for the last time in March of 1997, when he designed a pillbox hat (Diana's favorite style) that was worn with a pale blue Chanel suit to Prince William's confirmation. The designer had seen Diana less frequently after her divorce and looked back on the time spent with the Princess fondly. "She was no longer Her Royal Highness, and of course everything had changed, so she didn't need hats. But she wanted a hat for the confirmation because she was going to be seen in public with her family and she wanted to look very good," he said. "Without having many royal appearances she was wearing clothes differently. I have a lovely photo of her in the same suit when she went to a hospital to receive some roses named after her. All those years of working for her were so special. She is irreplaceable."

During the eighties, Diana indulged her love of whimsical fashion. Her penchant for polka dots dated back to her first appearances as Princess of Wales. She could look extremely young in her spotted sportswear, like her Mondi skirt and matching anklets that she

In 1988, Diana arrived in Paris in head-to-toe Chanel. It was the first time she had worn clothing from the collection for an official engagement. From that point on, Diana would frequently wear Chanel privately and was often photographed in Chanel ready-to-wear and accessories after her divorce.

"She developed her own style as she got more comfortable with her body and making decisions."

wore to a polo match in 1986, or incredibly chic in her Victor Edelstein dress seen at Ascot that same year. Structured jackets with decorative trim had become another Diana signature, but sometimes the style could look almost like a costume. In 1987, she chose an ivory suit with elaborate gold braiding by Catherine Walker to greet King Fahd of Saudi Arabia. Worn with a pillbox hat, it resembled a drum majorette's uniform. But Diana must have been very pleased with the look. She wore it again a short time later for a parade at the Sandhurst Royal Military Academy. Fashion editors decried it as too gimmicky, but Diana clearly loved "theme dressing" and the sight of her among the cadets in her own "uniform" was both striking and endearing.

Privately around this time, Diana had begun wearing a number of styles from foreign designers like Valentino and Yves Saint Laurent. For a 1988 trip to Paris, she arrived in head-to-toe Chanel. She had never worn clothing by a French designer for an official engagement before and her hosts were thrilled with the gesture. From that point on, Diana would frequently wear Chanel in private and was often photographed in

Chanel ready-to-wear and accessories after her divorce.

After receiving a great deal of guidance from advisers like Anna Harvey and Richard Dalton, Diana had finally settled on a more tailored, streamlined look as she neared her thirtieth birthday. Colored tights (another look Diana is largely credited with popularizing) were replaced with black sheers or bare legs (often enhanced by self-tanners). Catherine Walker, largely credited with helping Diana create her signature look, was named Best British Couturiere in 1990. The designer's elongated silhouettes, particularly her coatdresses, were extremely flattering. Walker's innovative use of color, particularly the bold brights the Princess loved, helped make every outfit photogenic.

Tomasz Starzewski was another designer whose clothes Diana now favored. His signature suits and dresses with bejeweled buttons and bias-banded skirts were a favorite among the young royals, and the Princess owned several styles from his collection. "She was more of a ready-to-wear buyer than a couture buyer," said the designer, explaining that at the time Diana

ABOVE, As Diana began taking on more engagements, she sought out clothes that reflected her "working woman" status, like this pink suit by Tomasz Starzewski, worn during a 1991 trip to Canada. OPPOSITE, The Princess also enjoyed wearing the designer's more whimsical styles, like this black velvet jacket and multi-colored banded skirt.

preferred off-the-rack styles over custom-made clothes. "She would never, ever take a drawing. She'd have to try a sample on. If she liked it, that's when she would buy it. And then you would make it for her. And it's interesting, because what that meant was that you didn't make a mistake and she didn't commit herself to something that wouldn't possibly work out. Things either worked straight away or didn't work at all."

As Diana took on more engagements without her husband and became increasingly involved in her charity work, she began to want more serious-looking clothes. "At the time, she had a quite conservative look and you could do quite conservative clothes for her. She liked the image that she was someone that was 'on the job,'" says Starzewski, "and that was what she was. We did 'working clothes' and 'non-working clothes' as well. Right up until her death she was wearing dresses that we made six years ago. One was the red crepe de chine dress with the gold ram's-head buttons she bought in 1990. She wore my dresses for seven years because she was very, very comfortable in them. She wore that one to Wimbledon and she wore it in Bosnia." Diana felt most at ease in structured clothes that looked polished but never stiff, the kind of styles that Starzewski was known for. "The last thing she wore publicly from me was the white suit with navy piping that she wore for the 50th Anniversary V-J Day Parade in 1995."

Her choices in eveningwear also reflected a new level of sophistication. Diana now gravitated toward dresses that were clean-lined and simply stunning, wearing styles from Catherine Walker and Victor Edelstein with increasing frequency. Ball gowns had been replaced by sleek columns that accentuated her height and slender figure. Above-the-knee cocktail suits showed off her fabulous legs. Some of her favorite gowns included a pale

OPPOSITE, In 1987, Diana evoked movie-star glamour at Cannes in a pale blue silk chiffon evening dress by Catherine Walker. RIGHT, In an off-the-shoulder black beaded jacket with white satin collar and cuffs and velvet skirt by Bellville Sassoon and Lorcan Mullany, Diana looked modern and confident.

blue chiffon strapless dress by Walker that was said to have been inspired by Grace Kelly's elegant style. Diana fittingly chose it for an appearance at the Cannes Film Festival in 1987 and again for the London opening of *Miss Saigon* in 1989. Another striking Walker creation was a pink and white crepe de chine column dress worn to the opening night of *Swan Lake* at the London Coliseum in 1989. That same year Diana appeared at the British Fashion Awards and on a trip to Hong Kong in what was affectionately dubbed "The Elvis Dress," an ivory beaded strapless gown with cropped bolero jacket by Catherine Walker. The Princess so loved the dress that she also wore it to several film premieres.

Other subtle changes in her appearance also indicated a newfound confidence. In the summer of 1990, Diana asked hairstylist Sam McKnight how she could update her appearance. He suggested cutting her hair short and, on a whim, she agreed. The newly flattering style looked modern and sophisticated. Diana had always bitten her nails and went to great lengths to keep them out of view (most photographs of the Princess show her making a fist so as not to draw attention to them). But by the early nineties, she was proudly sporting red polish on newly manicured nails. "You did see this pretty girl developing," said Janet Filderman, Diana's facialist for eleven years. "You didn't just see a young girl and then a woman." Filderman watched Diana evolve from an unremarkable teenager into a strikingly beautiful woman. "When she was young, you wouldn't have said, 'Oh what a beauty.' The makeover happened gradually with her development as a woman. I remember her

LEFT, Diana chose a long, lean evening dress by Catherine Walker for the first night of *Swan Lake* in 1989. BELOW, She looked radiant in a black velvet strapless gown by Victor Edelstein. OPPOSITE, Diana had become the royal family's most glamorous icon. This was plainly apparent during her 1989 appearances at the British Fashion Awards and in Hong Kong. For both occasions she chose one of her most stunning gowns: the beaded "Elvis" dress and jacket by Catherine Walker.

While Diana's royal "uniform"—a Catherine Walker suit and Philip Somerville hat like this one worn on a royal tour of Cairo in 1992—fit her perfectly, she had clearly outgrown her role as a "model" wife for Prince Charles.

Diana had begun wearing styles from international designers for select public appearances. In 1992, she attended Princess Eugenie's christening at Sandringham in this chic Moschino suit.

Prince Charles could never
compete with Diana's glamour.
That, among many other factors, contributed to the breakdown of their marriage. By
the end of 1992, the public's
desire for every detail of
Diana's style eclipsed virtually
everything any other royal did.

walking in here one day and I said, 'God, you're a woman.' And she looked at me with a twinkle in her eye and said, 'How do you know?' And I said, 'I could just tell.' She developed her own style as she got more comfortable with her body and with making her own decisions. She'd ask masses of people for advice but in the end, she'd go with her own gut feelings."

Diana was recognized for her contributions to fashion when she was named to the 1991/1992 International Best Dressed List's Hall of Fame for "having established an appropriate, non-dowdy modern style of royal dressing and bringing world recognition to young British designers." Her streamlined sheaths and two-piece suits with impeccably tailored long jackets could hardly be considered cutting-edge fashion, but on Diana they looked incredibly chic. The Princess's distinctive style was evident whenever she wore something from non-British designers in public, as she did when she selected a boldly patterned Moschino suit for Princess Eugenie's christening. After ten years of experimentation, she had seemingly mastered the art of royal dressing. Diana developed a formula for her clothes that fit her lifestyle and let her vibrant personality shine through. One of the things that set her apart from the rest of the royal family was her unerring eye when it came to accessories. Everything from hats to handbags to shoes was always perfectly coordinated and incredibly stylish.

When Diana and Charles first married both the press and the public were fascinated with the new Princess of Wales, and the royal family welcomed all the positive publicity. But as time went on, the public's desire for every detail of Diana's style from her clothes to her hair overshadowed virtually all other news about the royals. This is one of the many factors that contributed to the breakdown of Diana's marriage. Charles could never compete with Diana's glamour or convey the same sense of empathy that seemed to connect her to the world. Diana seemed to delight in upstaging her husband in subtle (and not-so-subtle) ways.

In 1992, the publication of *Diana: Her True Story* seemed to signal that the marriage was indeed over. By the end of that year, the announcement of an official separation confirmed it. But despite rumors that she had become unstable and was headed for a nervous breakdown, Diana appeared strong and in control. She was in search of a way to reinvent herself as a woman of both substance and style. The Princess had happily taken on the job of championing British fashion at the beginning of the eighties, but she was now making a concerted effort to re-focus the attention of the media on more substantive issues. Diana came to recognize that the tremendous attention that was paid to her wardrobe was diverting interest away from what she called "the Work." Determined not to be upstaged by her own glamour, she stopped issuing press releases that included details about her clothes. But that didn't mean she looked any less fabulous. In fact, she never looked better.

3
BREAKING AWAY

It is often said that a woman scorned heads for the gym or changes her hairstyle. Diana did both. While her newfound freedom must have been emotionally daunting, outwardly she appeared stronger than ever before. In early 1993, in what could be interpreted as a definitive show of empowerment, she intensified her already grueling fitness regimen of swimming, tennis and dance with regular trips to the L. A. Fitness Club. The results of her workouts were plainly evident: her once willowy frame had become more athletic and sensuous. One month after the official separation of Charles and Diana had been announced, she showed off her stunning figure (which now measured 36-26-36) during a Caribbean holiday on the beaches of Nevis by donning a series of bikinis and sophisticated one-piece styles from Gottex and Jantzen. During her marriage she had learned that her appearance was her most effective tool in communicating with the world. One look at Diana frolicking in the surf and the message was startlingly explicit: she was breaking away from the stifling atmosphere that had tried to silence her. She was going to enjoy being on her own.

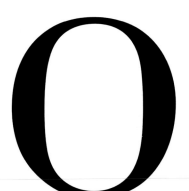

One of the most interesting aspects of Diana's appearance in the period following her separation was that she seemed to move effortlessly between two decidedly different wardrobes: one for her now limited appearances as part of the royal family, and one for those occasions when she felt freer to be herself. While protocol continued to dictate that Diana dress in suits and hats for formal state occasions, she managed to infuse even more of her personal style into the most structured clothes. Although seemingly less restricted by the royal rules, she remained sensitive to what was fitting and appropriate. The higher heels (the stilettos would come later), shorter skirts and gamin haircut were subtle signs of her emerging sense of freedom.

Diana was also becoming more and more adept at using clothes to shine the spotlight on herself whenever she deemed to do so. After the Queen declined to let Diana accompany her to Royal Ascot, the social event of the season, the Princess managed to upstage her mother-in-law just days before by showing up at the Order of the Garter ceremony in a shocking pink Catherine Walker suit. Its hemline showed more of Diana's great legs than had been seen before. She donned the requisite hat and gloves but looked anything but frumpy. With all eyes riveted on Diana everywhere she went, nothing she did—or wore—went unnoticed. Any official function she now attended turned into a fashion event.

The year following her separation proved to be a very difficult one for Diana and in December of 1993 she made an emotional speech announcing her decision to withdraw from most of her public duties. She now spent much of her free time on treatments that nourished her body and soul. Her daily schedule consisted of 7 a.m. visits to the gym (where she lifted weights) and workouts with personal trainer Carolan Brown, who often came to Kensington Palace to coach Diana in a vigorous routine of step aerobics. (She was horrified when photographs of her taken with a hidden camera at L. A. Fitness were published in

PREVIOUS PAGE, On holiday in Saint Barthelemy in 1995, Diana looked fit and fashionable. Everything about her seemed to convey that she was glad to be on her own.

OPPOSITE, Diana was the first royal to be photographed in workout clothes. Dashing from the gym in 1995, she wore a sweatshirt promoting more than British fashion. THIS PAGE, The results of her intense workouts were evident in Nevis in January of 1993.

In a pink Catherine Walker suit and a hat by Marina Killery, Diana looked both stylish and royal at the Order of the Garter ceremony in June of 1993.

the tabloids. Diana immediately switched to the exclusive Chelsea Harbour Club in June of 1993, where she worked out three mornings a week until her death.) Among the most enduring images of Diana are those that show her striding purposefully to the gym—car keys in hand—wearing her favorite sweatshirt and bicycle shorts. She was the first royal to be photographed in such casual attire—and she boosted the sale of whatever activewear label (including Polo Sport) that she chose to wear in the process. Other daily appointments included morning sessions with her hairdresser Sam McKnight as well as back-to-back New Age treatments like aromatherapy with Sue Beechey at Aromatherapy Associates in Fulham and colonic irrigation at the Hale Clinic in Regent Park. There were also weekly visits to her therapist Susie Orbach and her masseur Stephen Twigg. During this period of transition, she also frequently called on various faith healers and astrologers.

Shopping was another way Diana filled the empty hours. She was frequently spotted in Knightsbridge at many of her favorite designer shops carrying a leather notebook that she used to record her purchases. She also enjoyed shopping in the United States, where she was often the guest of Lucia Flecha de Lima, wife of the Brazilian ambassador to the U. S., who lived in Washington, D. C. On one shopping expedition with her friend in January of 1994, Diana visited Saks Fifth Avenue, Neiman-Marcus and a few other stores in the tony suburb of Chevy Chase, Maryland. Her purchases for the day were extremely modest. After perusing racks and racks of designer clothes, Diana settled on a pair of five-pocket jeans in a size 6 for $48 at Banana Republic.

In the early months of 1994, many veteran Diana watchers speculated that she had begun to veer dangerously toward the aimless existence of a bored socialite. Some critics sneered that she had merely exchanged one compulsion, bulimia, for a host of others: excessive exercise and compulsive spending on beauty treatments and clothes. Those speculations gained momentum when Diana's "grooming bills" were leaked to the press in what amounted to a calculated effort to paint her as a frivolous, self-centered woman. It was falsely reported that she spent in excess of $200,000 a year on her appearance. Diana countered by saying that her expenses in this area amounted to less than half that figure. Much of what she did spend was, under the terms of her separation, paid for by the Duchy of Cornwall. But Diana herself paid for most of her therapies and beauty treatments out of her own bank account. Unlike many celebrities who barter for free services and designer clothes in exchange for letting companies promote their affiliation with famous clients, Diana always made sure everything she bought was paid for. She was also religious about writing notes to designers to thank them for their efforts, and would often sit down at her desk still wearing the dress she had just received to effusively compliment its creator.

The Princess may have been indulging her passion for fashion after her separation, but she was loathe to let it define—or undermine—her. By the second half of 1994, she had defied the naysayers yet again. Diana was not becoming a lady who lunched and shopped. Under the watchful eye of Sir Robert Fellowes—the Queen's private secretary and husband of Diana's sister,

As a definitive show of empowerment, she intensified her already grueling fitness regimen.

Jane—she gradually began to take on an increasing number of public engagements. A stronger, more fortified Diana planned official trips to Paris and Japan. No formal announcement was made that the Princess had decided to reemerge from self-imposed semi-seclusion. No words were needed to communicate the news to the world; in many instances Diana let her wardrobe to do the talking. The daring dress designed by Christina Stambolian that she wore to the Serpentine Gallery in June of 1994 had certainly proven that.

"One Saturday, Diana and her brother came into my shop on Beauchamp Place," remembers Stambolian. Before that time, Diana had only worn clothing by the designer that she bought off-the-peg. "In the early eighties I saw her on a television program wearing a dress I designed, quite possibly bought from one of the boutiques I supplied at the time. It was long, in a bottle-green velvet with a wrap-around skirt. I was so excited to see her in one of my designs and proud that she looked so elegant." When Diana visited Stambolian's shop in 1994, the designer was thrilled to be on hand to personally help the Princess while Earl Spencer looked on. "She had a look around and bought a short red wool dress and a sleeveless silk blouse. Then she said she wanted something for a special occasion. We sat down and talked about it." When the designer suggested a short black dress with deep décolletage, Diana was not convinced at first that the revealing style was appropriate. "I thought that there should be less dress and more Diana because she was so beautiful," said Stambolian. "She was always wonderfully dressed but a lot of times I felt it wasn't her. Many of the dresses were too heavy and too much. At the time she wasn't very daring. She told me it was too short and too bare."

Finally, said Stambolian, "After a great deal of laughter and a nod from her brother, who thought she should do as she wanted, I convinced her the dress would be sensational. She said, 'Yes, let's be daring.' Then we deliberated further over the color, off-white or black. She thought off-white was too pale. It had to be one or the other because, with her, everything was black and white anyway." The two women settled on black

Diana was frequently spotted around London during her endless rounds of appointments. Off to her therapist Susie Orbach in December of 1995, she carried a leather-bound notebook to record her purchases.

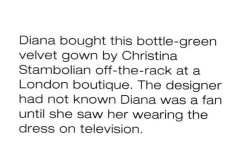

Diana bought this bottle-green velvet gown by Christina Stambolian off-the-rack at a London boutique. The designer had not known Diana was a fan until she saw her wearing the dress on television.

and the specially ordered silk jacquard fabric was flown in from Como, Italy. The dress with a small floral pattern on the bodice and a silk chiffon skirt with an attached scarf was made according to Diana's measurements. Ten days after the final fitting, the dress was delivered to Kensington Palace.

Although Diana had said the dress was to be worn at a special occasion, Stambolian hadn't known which occasion the Princess had in mind. Diana had already visited Valentino's London boutique where she mentioned she was looking for something to wear for the Serpentine gala. Just a few days before the event, Valentino had announced that Diana would be wearing one of his designs on that evening. Whether she was annoyed by the designer's premature bulletin or she simply changed her mind at the last minute, Diana opted for Stambolian's dress. ("I'm sure she didn't have in mind to wear my dress at that particular time," said Stambolian.) It was a stunning choice. The anything-but-basic little black dress fired a shot (at Charles and his court) heard around the world. While the Prince was confessing to adultery on national television, Diana had managed to upstage him once again simply by showing up–dressed to thrill.

While Diana had made many friends in the fashion industry since becoming Princess of Wales, it wasn't until January of 1995 that its international community truly welcomed her as one of their own. *Harper's Bazaar* editor Liz Tilberis had met Diana in 1987 when she became editor-in-chief of British *Vogue*. It was Tilberis

that brought together the venerable team of photographer Patrick Demarchelier, hairstylist Sam McKnight, and makeup artist Mary Greenwell that resulted in some of the most memorable images ever taken of the Princess. (Diana liked Demarchelier's work so much that she selected him to photograph her with her sons at Highgrove.) In 1991, Demarchelier was commissioned to photograph Diana for an issue of British *Vogue* celebrating The English National Ballet, of which Diana was a patron. For the sitting she had worn a simple black turtleneck and leggings. The Princess helped select the final images of herself that were to appear in the magazine. The most famous and compelling of the group was a close-up of Diana with her hands clasped under her chin. The startling photograph proved that she was the biggest fashion star ever to grace *Vogue's* cover. She looked more glamorous than any supermodel or film star.

When Tilberis moved to New York in 1992 for her new job as editor of *Harper's Bazaar*, the two women stayed in touch. Toward the end of 1993, Tilberis was diagnosed with ovarian cancer and Diana was one of a small number of people that knew about her illness. The two women came to have an intensely close friendship, one that would last for the rest of Diana's life. Sadly, Diana was not able to fulfill the promise she made just days before her death, to write the foreword to Tilberis's autobiography.

When the Council of Fashion Designers of America (CFDA) informed Tilberis that she was to receive an award at the organization's annual gala in January of 1995, she needed to select a presenter. Tilberis asked Diana. Much to her delight the Princess accepted. It was the first time

Diana appeared at a major fashion event outside of Britain. All of New York's fashion elite, including Ralph Lauren, Donna Karan and Calvin Klein, lined up to meet Diana. She chose a navy crepe backless sheath dress with eye-catching criss-cross straps by Catherine Walker for the event. "It elevated our show to a whole different level," said Stan Herman, president of the CFDA. "There was this gasp from the crowd when she appeared—and this is a group that has seen it all. It was amazing to see all these celebrities clamoring to get a look at Diana." Fully aware that the eyes of the fashion world were upon her, Diana decided to have some fun with her look. She transformed her usual layered bob into a sleek, slicked-back hairstyle minus her trademark bangs and wore one of her favorite pieces of jewelry, a multi-strand pearl choker adorned with a diamond and Sri Lankan sapphire brooch. The effect was dazzling.

As she walked across the stage to make the presentation to Tilberis there was a thunderous ovation. Someone in the audience shouted, "Move to New York!" Diana looked up into the crowd and smiled for a moment before beginning her remarks. It was the first time she had made a speech in the United States, and yet she managed to wow one of the most unflappable audiences imaginable. That night, the international fashion community caught the same Di-fever that millions of people around the world had been nurturing for years. She had become the most important and influential client any designer could hope to have.

Long before she lost her royal title, Diana had already abandoned most of the pomp and circumstance of royal dressing. As she started to feel more empowered physically and emotionally, she began to disregard the stifling dress codes adopted during her married life and let her personal glamour shine through. The "Shy Di" who tilted her head down and cast sidelong glances to the camera was a distant memory. Now Diana gazed directly at photographers when she made a public appearance. At 5'10", she stood even taller with her newly perfect posture. No longer worried about towering over Prince Charles, she happily exchanged her low-heeled

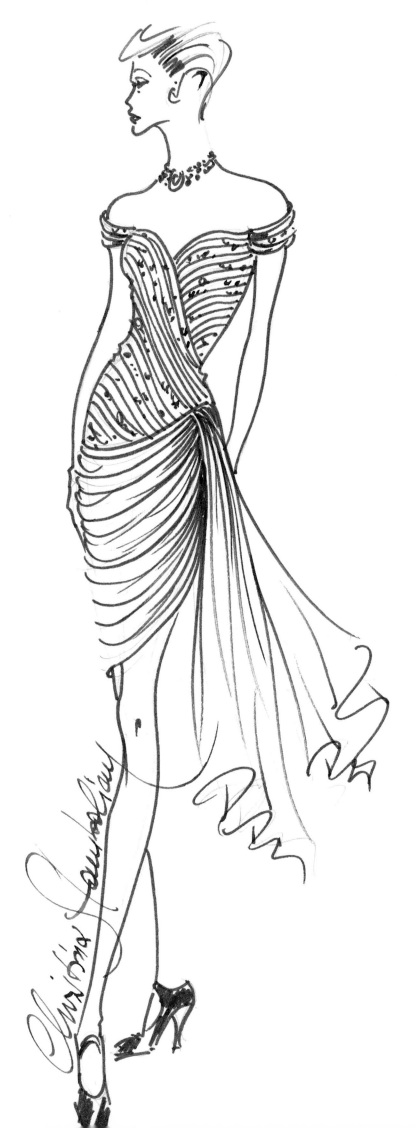

OPPOSITE, Diana's clothes spoke louder than words when she appeared at London's Serpentine Gallery in this dramatic black dress by Christina Stambolian. On the same night in June of 1994, Charles was confessing to adultery on national television. LEFT, A sketch of Diana in the same dress.

"There was this gasp from the crowd when she appeared —and this was a group that has seen it all."

In New York in 1995 to present her friend, *Harper's Bazaar* editor Liz Tilberis, with an award from the Council of Fashion Designers of America, Diana turned heads with her dramatic slicked-back hairstyle.

pumps for the sexy spike heels of Manolo Blahnik and Jimmy Choo. She radiated a new, more vibrant energy. Many of those who traveled with her had to literally run to keep up with her. Her style had been transformed from somewhat sweet, safe and traditional to fresh and modern. While she had sometimes been labeled a fashion victim in the earlier years, it became increasingly clear that those fashion mistakes only happened when she was trying to dress by the rules that governed the rest of the royals. Diana as herself was stunning and very sophisticated.

Just as the formal suits and hats from her faithful coterie of British designers had become emblematic of her royal role, the increasing number of body-conscious styles she chose to wear in 1995 from foreign designers–particularly Gianni Versace, whose designs she had been wearing in private since 1991–effectively illustrated the independent woman Diana had become. Her decision to wear Versace's clothes represented an important milestone for Diana. She had reached a point in her style–and her life–where she was comfortable with her sexuality. While the designer's suits were sleek and understated, his evening clothes, with their intricate boning and impeccable tailoring, showed off every curve of Diana's figure to perfection. And just as Versace's clothes played a role in creating the Princess's new modern look, she in turn became somewhat of a muse for him. In order to dress the Princess, he toned down his outrageously flamboyant designs to suit her. The influence of Diana's newly-minted style was subtly present in the designer's subsequent collections.

Her wardrobe was now full of classically tailored separates by Ralph Lauren, as well as day and evening looks from Karl Lagerfeld for Chanel and from Christian Lacroix. (Diana was also an admirer of Hervé Leger's stunning designs, though she declined to wear anything from his collections out of consideration for Viscountess Linley, who wore Leger quite often.) But Diana had not deserted British fashion entirely. She had simply edited down her wardrobe to include only the most flattering clothes that she liked best. Catherine Walker remained largely responsible for her daytime looks and many of her evening gowns. Diana also remained faithful to Jacques Azagury, whose dresses for her would continue to grow increasingly daring.

Diana was a frequent visitor to many of London's toniest boutiques, where she would often arrive unannounced to peruse the racks filled with the latest styles. She would regularly shop on Beauchamp Place (a favorite haunt since she had first begun visiting Bruce Oldfield and Caroline Charles in the very early days after her wedding) before lunching with friends at one of her favorite restaurants, San Lorenzo. "She never liked to tell us the time she was coming," said Christina Stambolian. "She just popped in." The only time Diana would make an appointment was when she needed a fitting for a specific dress. At Versace's London boutique, she would come for private fittings for couture dresses, then browse through the store examining his ready-to-wear collection while other clients looked on slightly awestruck. Aware that her presence often resulted in a commotion, Diana frequently engaged the services of Gabriella Di Nora, a personal shopper at Harvey

At the CFDA dinner with Tilberis at her side, Diana won over the "seen-it-all" New York fashion crowd, in a navy crepe gown with an open back by Catherine Walker. It was the first time she spoke publicly in America.

LEFT, In Paris in September of 1995 Diana received a Lady Dior bag from the First Lady of France, Bernadette Chirac, that became an instant status symbol. OPPOSITE, The Princess loved the bag and wore it frequently. Here, she paired it with a boldly colored suit from Catherine Walker.

Nichols. The Princess had been coming to the store long before her wedding and still stopped by to pick up Annick Goutal Passion (her signature scent), Donna Karan hosiery and cosmetics from Clinique. At Harrods, the highly efficient and discreet staff would often receive a call from Diana's lady-in-waiting asking for an escort for the Princess or requesting that certain items (often La Perla lingerie) be ready for her in a private shopping area.

In November of 1995, when Diana visited Paris for the opening of the Cézanne show, Bernadette Chirac, the First Lady of France, gave her a Lady Dior handbag which was named for Diana and cost $1,100. She fell in love with the bag and was frequently photographed carrying several different versions, each with its signature and anything-but-subtle gilt letters that spelled out DIOR. (During her marriage Diana usually carried unadorned, generally non-descript bags.) Virtually overnight, the Princess's royal seal of approval catapulted the bag into the fashion stratosphere as *the* must-have accessory of the moment. It sold out all over Europe and there was a worldwide waiting list for the newly minted status symbol. Once again, Diana had (intentionally or not) given women a tangible way (albeit through an extremely expensive emblem) to imitate her style. They may not be able to have her face, figure or Dior couture gown, but they could carry the bag—*her* bag. In fact, women asked for the style by the name they had given it: the "Lady Di." And for those who could not afford the $1,200 price tag that the bag now sported, there was a bumper crop of instant imitators to choose from.

Diana's sense of style and an ability to dress in clothing that complemented — and was complemented — by her surroundings (here in two dresses by Catherine Walker) made every photo call suitable for the pages of a fashion magazine.

Diana wore this glamorous low-cut gown by Jacques Azagury to a London gala held on the same evening her famous BBC interview was being televised. One month later pictured here, she appeared in the stunner again to receive an award in New York.

At 34, she was an accessible icon— someone women could both sympathize with and aspire to be like.

For millions of women around the world, their growing personal connection and sense of kinship with Diana was due in large part to her shattering performance during her November 1995 interview with Martin Bashir of the BBC's "Panorama." Looking nervous and drawn, she openly discussed her disappointment in a failed marriage, her battle with "rampant bulimia," her struggles with low self-esteem and her strong desire to survive and thrive against seemingly overwhelming obstacles. None of this diminished her. Describing her newfound freedom and life after the separation, she said, "People think that at the end of the day, a man is the only answer. Actually, a fulfilling job is better for me." At 34, she was an accessible icon—someone women could both sympathize with and aspire to be like. This proved to be a thoroughly intoxicating combination that increased her star power exponentially.

Although women identified with Diana in ways that extended far beyond her style, her influence on fashion was now at an all-time high. Jacques Azagury first met Diana in 1985 when Anna Harvey introduced them at a London fashion show. Diana wore several things from his collection from that point on, but it was the black low-cut dress which she wore to a gala in London on the same night her now-famous "Panorama" interview aired that earned Azagury a place in the Princess's small circle of favorite designers. She also appeared in the dress one month later in New York when she received the Humanitarian Award at the Annual United Cerebral Palsy Awards Dinner. "That was the first dress we did that was seriously body-conscious," said Azagury. "When I showed it to her, she said, 'That's a bit of a sexy dress, Jacques'—and I said, 'Yes.' Then she tried it on and she loved it. I think she was treating it as kind of a 'result' dress. That very night she was on "Panorama" telling the whole world what was happening in her life. She wanted a dress that would go, 'Wow!' I think the interview was still on when she was arriving at

the gala, so the press went mad. She wanted a really sexy dress and it was her way of saying, 'Look, I'm free, almost single and I'm a woman.'"

While she enthralled a huge television audience (the program aired on the Queen's 48th wedding anniversary) with tales of a marriage gone wrong looking pale and wan, her glamorous alter-ego was dazzling the hordes of photographers and onlookers. It was simply another instance where she had to put her feelings of insecurity and unhappiness aside and become 'Princess Diana.' In many ways she was at her most radiant dressed up in glamorous gowns for an adoring public, and that evening was no exception. "I saw her the day before the interview aired and I asked her if she was nervous," Azagury remembers. "She said, 'I've done nothing wrong; I'm not nervous at all. I've said nothing damaging.' On television, she looked very, very nervous but I think she was pleased she did it."

Although Diana never set out to be a fashion icon, she was fully aware that her sense of style was an important part of her allure. During a 1995 fitting with milliner Philip Somerville, the Princess made what has proven to be a prescient reference to her connection to another fashion legend. "She was trying on a hat," said Somerville, recalling the pink pillbox he had designed to coordinate with a Versace suit. "When I saw the outfit I thought it was very Jackie Kennedy. Then she said, 'I wonder if in the years to come people will think of me as the Jackie Kennedy of the period.' She admired Mrs. Kennedy and I think what she said has now come true." It is interesting to note that Jackie was equally intrigued by Diana. In *Jackie After Jack*, biographer Christopher Anderson writes that Jackie thought Diana was "beautiful, elegant, charming, very stylish and a wonderful mother." While an editor at Doubleday, Jackie pursued the Princess in hopes of getting her to agree to write her autobiography. Diana's office at Buckingham Palace rejected the offer.

In the realm of style, it is clear that both women have attained mythic stature. Having set

Diana wore an increasing number of styles by foreign designers after her separation. OPPOSITE, She chose this striking red cocktail dress by Christian Lacroix for a visit to Le Petit Palais in Paris. RIGHT, She still remained loyal to her favorite British designers, like Jacques Azagury, who designed this two-piece beaded dress worn in Venice one month earlier.

LEFT, Diana loved the sleek, clean-lined designs of Gianni Versace, like the one she wore in September of 1995 to a concert given by her friend Luciano Pavarotti. OPPOSITE, Another striking Versace dress, worn during her trip to Australia.

an impossibly high standard by which women around the world, consciously or not, measure their own appearance, persona and self-esteem, Diana and Jackie both possessed an almost magical, indefinable star quality. There are many intriguing similarities in the lives of Diana and Jackie: both dealt with unrelenting world attention at a young age, raised families in the spotlight and went on to redefine themselves several times during the course of their lives. But it is Diana's incandescent inner and outer beauty that has elevated her beyond every other fashion icon—including Jackie—that came before her.

Diana lived two lives. Publicly, she was the most glamorous, celebrated woman in the world and in private, she was heartbreakingly lonely. As divorce loomed, she seemed determined to bridge the gap between the two. Her fame—and her glamour—had become her most valuable tool in positioning herself as a woman capable of surviving on her own. In June of 1996, a three-day trip to Chicago proved how determined Diana was to establish herself as a humanitarian figure. The purpose of the Princess's visit was to raise money for three cancer charities: Northwestern University's Robert H. Lurie Center, Gilda's Club, a support network for women with cancer founded by Gene Wilder in honor of his late wife, actress Gilda Radner and London's Royal Marsden Hospital, of which Diana was president. This was clearly a working trip for the Princess, but one that also sparkled with Diana's unique brand of glamour.

Ann Jackson, publisher of *InStyle* magazine, accompanied Diana for much of the trip. "I basically saw her every day from seven in the morning until eleven o'clock at night. She didn't change her clothes—she just wore one thing during the day and one thing at night like any of us would," said Jackson. "But there was something about her—there was never a wrinkle or a spot. She looked totally fabulous having marched around Northwestern's campus. The hair was

Diana had already abandoned the pomp and circumstance of royal dressing. As she started to feel more empowered physically and emotionally, she began to let her personal glamour shine through.

perfect and so was the makeup. The first night she was brought to a small reception at the President's house. She had just done a tour of the campus and it was raining. She walked in the door in a pale green Catherine Walker suit with perfectly matching shoes. The suit had a long jacket of the sort she often wore. She looked like she just stepped out of a salon. It was as if the rain drops hadn't even touched her. She had this beautiful little bouquet of either violets or lilies of the valley that someone had given her. When she entered the room, you immediately felt her presence. Right away you could see her remarkable charm. She never appeared to be rushed. When she walked into the house she probably had fifty or so people to speak to, but when she was speaking to you it was as if you were the only person on the planet and she had all the time in the world."

Jackson remembers how on the second night of the tour, Diana wowed the crowds at a black-tie fund-raiser at Chicago's Natural History Museum by showing up in a purple Versace gown. "Northwestern's school color is purple and everyone thought how wonderful she had chosen it," said Jackson. "The truth was it was completely unplanned on her part. I said to her, 'Just tell them you knew.' She laughed. But it was really just a nice coincidence. She walked down some beautiful marble stairs at the beginning of the dinner after a private reception, and except for the fact

that she always bowed her head a little bit, her presence was beautiful and somewhat regal."

On the final day of the trip, everyone was completely exhausted—except Diana. "Again she got up early in the morning after the dinner—where she drank only water. I think she was very disciplined. It was the only way she could keep up that kind of schedule," said Jackson. "After the black-tie dinner she went to a swimming pool at the hotel, which had been quietly arranged, and swam for an hour." Diana also kept in shape by using an exercise bicycle she had requested for her room at the Drake Hotel. "She hadn't gone to bed until twelve or one, and she was up again at 6:30 or 7 o'clock to do some more touring. She didn't just want to see the research facilities and the sort of hospitals where the rich people go, she wanted to see the inner cities." That day at her good-bye luncheon Diana radiated confidence and serenity in a sleeveless white Versace dress. Jackson marveled at her stamina and grace. "I said to her, 'How do you do this?' I've been keeping up with half your schedule and I'm completely exhausted. You must have shaken a thousand hands in the last three days; met a thousand people. And she said to me, 'This is the easy part. The hard part is tomorrow night when I'm home in an empty house.' She was very easy to be with. She certainly never seemed arrogant in the least. There was a certain humility about her."

Without the frills and flourishes of her royal wardrobe, Diana was the quintessence of pared-down chic. She was spotted leaving Raine Spencer's London home in a pale blue Versace suit and Gucci tote in August of 1996.

What made Diana's Chicago appearance all the more fascinating is that it took place just a few weeks before her divorce became final. Jackson remembers a conversation with Diana about Hillary Clinton that revealed much about how Diana perceived the treatment she was receiving in Britain at the time. "I asked her what she thought about Hillary Clinton and she said she admired her tremendously. Diana seemed to feel that she had some of the same problems Hillary did because she was such a strong person and she hadn't absolutely done what she was told to do. She said, 'You know, in England we are making progress, but women–independent women–have not made as much progress as they have in America. But someday we will.' She did say it was tough sometimes and she was very empathetic with Hillary."

Jackson then asked Diana how she sustained peace of mind while spending so much time with victims of serious illnesses and other tragedies. "She'd been to Pakistan the week before visiting a cancer hospital and I asked her didn't she ever get depressed? And she said, 'No, sitting on the edge of someone's bed in those situations is the least complicated relationship you can have in your life. They're happy to see you, you're happy to do whatever small amount you can do just by being there. And it's incredibly energizing. It's what keeps me going.'"

Diana wound up her stay in Chicago by making an impromptu speech to thank her hosts. "She had these perfect hand-written notes on her stationery, thanking everyone," said Jackson, who marveled at Diana's attention to detail. "She went over some of the names with me of famous people and dignitaries that she wanted to speak about before she got up, just to make sure she'd gotten it just right. Everyone was thrilled."

Jackson saw Diana for the last time one year later, in June of 1997, when she came to New York for the Christie's auction preview party sponsored by *InStyle.* She noticed a marked difference in Diana's demeanor. "She seemed more confident, happier, more grown-up than she had the year

Diana's signature look for day: simple yet impeccably tailored sheath dresses (these two are from Versace) worn with pearls. Looking more confident, she personified fashion's "less is more" mood of the moment.

By the mid-nineties, Diana's look was decidedly more modern and monied, as shown in this yellow suit worn with her Cartier watch.

Weeks before her divorce in June of 1996, Diana (shown here in a lime-colored suit by Catherine Walker) visited the campus of Northwestern University. Said *InStyle* magazine's Ann Jackson, who accompanied her on the trip, "She looked like she just stepped out of a couture salon."

before. Mostly more confident; she stood up a little straighter. The room was so crowded you could barely move but she was unfazed. Arnold Scassi said to her, 'Diana, you look beautiful.' And she said, 'Arnold are you saying divorce becomes me?' She was very capable of sophisticated repartee. She was great fun. When she walked into the room that night I said, 'I'm going to be interrupting you all night and introducing you to people, I hope you won't think it's rude.' She said, 'Absolutely not, I'm here to work. Just tell me what you want me to do.'"

In the months leading up to her divorce, Diana had become increasingly effective in her public role and spent more of her time doing work for those causes she believed in. She had found a formidable ally in the fashion industry. In September of 1996, she came to Washington, D. C. on her first solo visit since the divorce to help raise money for the Nina Hyde Center for Breast Cancer Research. Diana served as the honorary chair of the Breast Cancer Super Sale benefit, working alongside co-chairs *Vogue* editor-in-chief Anna Wintour, Chairman of the Executive Committee of The Washington Post Company, Katharine Graham and designer Ralph Lauren. Looking stunningly beautiful in a backless white lace gown by Catherine Walker, Diana stood out in a sea of black (the uniform color of choice by the fashionable crowd). That night she danced with Colin Powell, Oscar de la Renta and Calvin Klein (Diana reportedly joked that she liked his underwear). Other guests were deemed off-limits by Diana's co-hosts because they were too short, too young or unmarried. Once again surrounded by celebrities, politicians and supermodels, Diana had been the evening's brightest star.

OPPOSITE, Diana looked sexy and strong in this Catherine Walker coatdress worn with strappy pumps. ABOVE, In a black gown worn to the Serpentine Gallery, Diana demonstrated another kind of strength.

Diana (in a Catherine Walker suit) found many important allies for her charitable causes within the fashion industry. Besides dressing her for public and private occasions, Ralph Lauren became a good and trusted friend. The two shared an interest in raising money to fight breast cancer.

When Diana saw herself in this hat by Philip Somerville and suit from Versace, she was reminded of another revered fashion icon. "She loved pillboxes," said Somerville. "She brought her own youthful style to them and made them popular again."

"She was trying on a hat," said Somerville of the pink pillbox he designed. "She said, 'I wonder if in the years to come people will think of me as the Jackie Kennedy of the period.'"

For some time, Diana had been lunching regularly with editors of glossy fashion and lifestyle magazines. After her death, *Vogue's* Anna Wintour, *The New Yorker's* Tina Brown and *Harper's Bazaar's* Liz Tilberis all shared some of their "intimate" memories of the Princess through the pages of their magazines. What is most interesting about their accounts is that they each presented different sides of Diana's complex personality: the glamorous style icon, the serious humanitarian, the dutiful mother and the compassionate friend. Diana possessed a strong chameleon-like quality with an ability to assume the appropriate persona and demeanor for virtually any situation she was in. After many years of being a role model to millions of people around the world, in the two years prior to her death, she had earned the admiration of many of the world's most influential fashion editors, not only for her distinctive style, but for her humanity.

In December of 1996, Diana returned to New York to attend the Metropolitan Museum of Art's gala benefit for its Costume Institute, one of the most glamorous evenings of the city's winter social season. Once again, Diana had chosen to accompany Tilberis, the evening's chair, to a high-profile fashion event. Over 900 people paid $1,000 each to dine on sea bass and get a glimpse of Diana. This was the only time in recent memory that her fashion choice had met with mixed reviews. She wore the first dress from John Galliano's couture collection for Dior (she also carried a satin Lady Dior evening bag). While the fashion crowd heralded her choice as sophisticated and savvy, others felt the negligee-inspired gown was decidedly unroyal. Diana was clearly dabbling with the fashion-of-the-moment, something she didn't often do. It had been years since she'd fallen victim to trying a trend that didn't suit her. The slip dresses being worn by rail-thin models on the runways of Europe just didn't seemed suitable for a Princess. She looked better in more structured clothes. But Diana gamely donned the dress, partly out of respect for the House of Dior, which was being feted at the gala.

She reacted with characteristic good humor when she learned that the press had given her a less-than-enthusiastic review for her attire. She herself later admitted she had trouble keeping up the delicate lace straps of the bare gown. After the dinner Diana quietly slipped away, returning to her suite at the Carlyle Hotel (her favorite place to stay during her trips to New York), where she chatted with her sister Lady Sarah McCorquodale, who accompanied her on the overnight trip. Even when she stumbled a bit with her style, she still had the unrivaled ability to touch off a trend. By wearing the gown, Diana had given Galliano's collection unrivaled publicity and christened the slip dress "chic." Overnight it became a "must-have" for sophisticated haute couture customers around the world.

Diana
earned
the
admiration
of
fashion
editors
not only
for her
distinctive
style,
but for
her
humanity.

When Diana wore a navy slip dress from John Galliano's first couture collection for Dior to the Metropolitan Museum's Costume Institute gala in December of 1996, some decried her choice as more appropriate for a model than a princess. Never taking fashion all that seriously, Diana took the criticism in stride.

4

A WOMAN IN EARNEST

Almost from the very beginning, Diana had been adept at using clothes to tell her story, and never was that more apparent than during the last year of her life. Her style became symbolic of post-feminist dressing. Jacques Azagury, who designed the most overtly sexy dresses ever worn by the Princess, explained Diana's transformation this way: "In the last year of her life, her confidence, her well-being, everything came through in the clothes she was wearing. She was pleased to be who she was." Now, every time she appeared in public there was something about her appearance — whether it was a gown which revealed more cleavage than the one worn before it or a man-tailored pantsuit worn with a lacy camisole underneath—that seemed to say that she was free of the restrictions she had endured for so long and was much happier with herself as a result. Diana had found a way to dress—and live—to please herself. She had survived an existence that had been both superficial and restricting and had worn hundreds of suits, dresses and ball gowns that reflected it. At long last, Diana had honed her fashion sense to near perfection.

PREVIOUS PAGE, In 1997, Diana proved she had transcended fashion. Her classic beauty, vitality and humanity were truly the essence of her unique style.

Dressing to please herself, Diana began wearing more styles from foreign designers for public appearances. RIGHT, In one of her favorite Chanel suits holding a bouquet of the rose named after her. ABOVE, For lunches and appointments around London Diana often donned simple, man-tailored suits like this one, accessorized with pumps by Jimmy Choo and her J. P. Tod's shopping bag.

In 1997, Diana's look had become streamlined and simplified. Her hair was straighter and longer and blonder, her makeup softer and more natural (the long favored kohl-blue eyeliner was finally gone for good). Diana's body also reflected a new sense of confidence and contentment. Her once alarmingly bulimic frame that had at one time become almost too muscular, had now softened into a voluptuous womanly figure. No longer the dutiful ambassador of British fashion (or a wife trapped in a loveless marriage), she declared her independence by wearing an increasing number of Chanel suits and Versace dresses (although she still relied heavily on her good friend Catherine Walker for most of her "working" wardrobe). The suits she most often wore for daytime functions were without adornment, except for their extremely flattering and

But her uncomplicated approach to her style belied the complicated woman she clearly had become. Diana certainly looked sophisticated and sensual, but she also appeared more serious—and her earnestness showed in what she chose to wear both publicly and privately. She had long ago decided she didn't want to be a figurehead—to put on an evening dress, go to a benefit and later receive a thank-you and find out how much money had been raised. "I want to do, not just be," she told her friend Rosa Monckton. During her trip to Angola in January, where she spent most of her time comforting the victims of anti-personnel mines, she wore simple, crisp white shirts and khakis. They were, without question, the humblest clothes in her closet and, of course, entirely appropriate and universally understood. By the time she made the journey to Bosnia in April wearing similar clothing (albeit from Ralph Lauren and Emporio Armani), she had unwittingly created another signature Diana

Her uncomplicated approach to her style belied the complicated woman she had become. Diana looked sophisticated and sensual, but appeared more serious—and her earnestness showed in what she chose to wear.

photogenic color. The body-conscious gowns that revealed her innately modern beauty were almost always sheath dresses, her high-wattage celebrity providing virtually all of the sparkle. The only style holdover from her pre-divorce days was her penchant for large earrings and pearls and preference for structured designer handbags.

"She was following fashion on the fashion scale rather than the 'Princess' scale," said Azagury. Indeed, in wearing a Dior slip dress by John Galliano or carrying a Gucci or Dior bag, Diana was demonstrating her newfound status as a global figure and offered a glimpse into the international circles in which she now traveled with increasing frequency. Her wardrobe had become the perfect, impeccably chosen backdrop for what the world wanted to see: Diana as herself.

look. Even when fashion was the furthest thing from her mind, she could never escape her role as a style icon completely.

While Diana made a concerted effort to shed her clotheshorse image in the last years of her life, she also forged close relationships with several internationally known designers. She spent time with Ralph Lauren during her trips to the United States working to raise money for breast cancer research, she vacationed at Krizia designer Mariuccia Mandelli's K Club in Barbuda and socialized with Valentino aboard his yacht. Gianni Versace, who became a good friend and one of the Princess's favorite designers ("She is a dream client," he once said), learned that their fashionable friendship had its limits. Versace had asked Diana to pose for his new book, *Rock and Royalty*, and to be the guest of

The pared-down, minimalist look Diana perfected in the last year of her life. RIGHT, She continued to rely on Catherine Walker for many of her daytime suits. OPPOSITE, On vacation in August she radiated health and happiness in St. Tropez.

honor at a party to launch the book and to serve as a fund-raiser for The Elton John AIDS Foundation. The Princess happily agreed and even penned the book's foreword. In February, Diana learned that the London *Sunday Times* planned to run a cover story in its style section with the headline: "Exposed: How Diana, Princess of Wales, Slipped Between the Sheets with 30 Naked Men." When she finally saw a copy of the book, which included pictures of men wearing only towels and crowns juxtaposed with photographs of Queen Elizabeth and other royals, she withdrew her support and asked that her foreword also be withdrawn. Diana had accurately assessed that the negative publicity could do considerable damage to her new image of putting substance before style. Versace canceled the party and withdrew Diana's foreword while insisting there was nothing wrong with the book. The incident reportedly caused a rift between Diana and Elton John that ended at Versace's funeral in Milan in July, when the two put aside their differences to console each other over the loss of the designer.

Diana had specific goals for 1997. Publicly, she had decided to focus her energies on a specific number of charities and causes, while privately she wanted to put her past behind her and forge a rewarding and pleasurable future. The decision to have Christie's auction off seventy-nine of her dresses with the proceeds going to two charities, the Royal Marsden Hospital Cancer Fund and the AIDS Crisis Trust (both chosen by the Princess), seemed aimed at achieving both. "Words cannot adequately describe my absolute delight at the benefits which the results of this auction will bring to so many people who need support," said Diana in a press release on the event. "We should all

During her trips to Angola and Bosnia, Diana adopted a simple working wardrobe of crisp oxford shirts by Ralph Lauren, khakis and J. P. Tod's loafers.

share in the pleasure in being able to help in this way."

The sale, which Diana said was the idea of her eldest son, Prince William, was planned over the course of several months under a veil of great secrecy. Meredith Etherington-Smith, creative director of marketing at Christie's International and a former fashion editor of French *Vogue*, met with Diana at Kensington Palace and worked closely with her on every detail. During their earliest meetings, Diana even cataloged each dress herself, writing brief descriptions of each style in Etherington-Smith's notebook. Diana had selected artifacts from her past that spoke volumes about her life. With the help of her butler Paul Burrell, she led Etherington-Smith through an abridged oral history of life as Her Royal Highness as she pulled each dress from her wardrobe. Indeed, the Princess's life had been so well-documented during that period that these garments could easily be cross-referenced with the many significant events in her life. But seeing the dresses on exhibit made one thing perfectly clear: without Diana, there was no magic in these designs. It was the Princess that gave star power to the frothy confections like those by the Emanuels worn during her earliest years of marriage ("My fairy period," as Diana often described it). The daring Christina Stambolian "Take That, Camilla" dress that the Princess wore the night Prince Charles discussed his relationship with Camilla Parker Bowles on television, seemed even more audacious simply because Diana had worn it.

The clothes, a mixture of couture gowns and off-the-peg dresses worn to official state visits and functions (and all by British designers), needed to be photographed for the Christie's catalog. Having anyone other than Diana model them seemed out of the question. It was decided that the book would feature a mixture of shots of the dresses on couture dummies, with Diana modeling some of her favorites. Also included were large-format detail shots of the intricate sequins, beading and embroidery on many of the dresses that illustrated the craftsmanship of the designs. Diana chose Lord Snowdon, who had photographed her so many times over the years, for the catalog's portraits. The Princess also asked Sam McKnight, the hairdresser who had created the short, cropped style she began wearing in the early nineties, and makeup artist Mary Greenwell, to work on the shoot. The resulting photographs showed a clearly more mature

Diana chose clothes that clearly conveyed her respect for her hosts. For example, OPPOSITE, she wore a simple white suit when she met with Mother Teresa in New York. ABOVE, Diana observed Islamic protocol in a salwaar kameez by Geeta Sarin for her visit to Imran Khan's cancer hospital and research center in Pakistan.

The photographs captured an intriguing combination of the old and new Diana.

Diana, looking somewhat subdued and strained but undeniably beautiful.

These photographs captured an intriguing combination of the old and new Diana. Perhaps that is why she doesn't look entirely comfortable. In choosing Lord Snowdon, the former husband of Princess Margaret, for the project, it seemed as if Diana instinctively knew his lens would capture both the regal and restrictive mood of the clothes. According to Etherington-Smith, who wrote about her experience with the Princess and the auction in *The Mail on Sunday*, after the Snowdon shoot the Princess thought it might be a good idea to take more photographs with a new photographer. Etherington-Smith suggested fashion photographer Mario Testino, whose youthful, energetic images frequently graced the pages of *Vogue*. The photographs from that shoot (Diana's last), which appeared in the July 1997 issue of *Vanity Fair*, were a stark contrast to Snowdon's work. Diana looked more like an exuberant fashion model than a princess. She had completed her final transformation into a thoroughly modern woman and had chosen to document the watershed event for all the world to see.

In June, Diana attended gala previews of "Dresses," the straightforward name that Etherington-Smith gave the sale, with Diana's approval. Parties were held in New York and London. Both events brought out scores of Diana-watchers, as well as many of the designers whose creations were part of the sale. Elizabeth Emanuel, David Sassoon, Jacques Azagury and

OPPOSITE, At the New York preview of "Dresses," Diana chose a Catherine Walker beaded dress and her favorite pair of Jimmy Choo shoes for the occasion. TOP, The Victor Edelstein dress which sold for $222,500—the highest price ever paid for a garment at auction. MIDDLE, Snowdon photographed Diana modeling several dresses for the auction's catalog, including this ballerina-style gown by Murray Arbeid.

RIGHT, Catherine Walker's "Elvis" dress was a highly sought-out favorite.

*As the most enduring fashion icon
of the modern age,
Diana was the woman
that millions of women wanted
to look at and look like.*

Christina Stambolian attended the London preview. Diana looked dazzling in an ice-blue Catherine Walker cocktail dress and enjoyed chatting with the designers. "She was full of life, looked wonderful and extremely happy," said Stambolian. "I told her so and she giggled. She was always giggling. I remember her bending down because she was so tall and I am so small and whispering to me, 'I really had to squeeze myself into that dress.' She always downplayed herself; she always maintained a sense of humor." David Sassoon, who designed Diana's trousseau and much of her wardrobe in the early years of her marriage, asked the Princess what became of one of her favorite dresses, the going-away outfit he had designed for her. "She smiled and said, 'Oh, I'm holding on to that one.'"

Catherine Walker also attended the London event and spent much of the evening in conversation with Diana. Walker holds the distinction of being the only designer to have dressed Diana throughout the entire period of her public life. An extremely close friend and confidante of the Princess, Walker shared a bond with her that few people did. Both women were the same height, size and astrological sign (Cancer). Together they devised a formula for Diana's

wardrobe that rarely, if ever, failed her. Equally important to their relationship was the support they offered each other in their personal lives. When Walker learned she had breast cancer in 1995, Diana was there for her. "I have received unfailing support from the Princess of Wales since I was diagnosed with the disease," said Walker. "I am therefore deeply moved that my designs, through the Princess, are now being used to save lives."

Footwear designer Jimmy Choo, who had met Diana through designer Tomasz Starzewski, was pleased to see the Princess had chosen to wear one of his styles at the New York pre-auction party. Choo had been making couture shoes for Diana for seven years and said she owned so many pairs from him that he lost count of the actual number. Diana frequently called on the designer when she wanted something made to coordinate with a particular gown or suit, as she did when she commissioned him to create the elegant purple heels she wore with her stunning Versace gown in Chicago. Her extensive footwear wardrobe contained a mixture of Choo's pumps and flats. "Her favorites were high-heel strappy shoes," Choo recalled. "She liked classic styles—she never wore sandals. The shoes she wore to

Diana looked sensational in a scarlet beaded Jacques Azagury gown at a Red Cross benefit with Elizabeth Dole in June of 1997.

Azagury's powder-
blue mini was one of
the most daring dress-
es Diana ever wore.
"It matched her eyes
perfectly," said the
designer.

the auction were four years old and still looked good."
Choo, who said Diana always helped him pack up his
trunks and carry his cases to his car after every
appointment, remembers her as his best customer.
"She was never fussy and never complained. She
always paid her bill on time, was very easy to deal
with and always knew what she wanted. Whenever I
brought shoes to her, she would run to Paul [Burrell,
her butler] and say, 'Look at these beautiful shoes
Jimmy has made for me.'" The Malaysian-born
designer was to deliver the last pair of shoes he made
for Diana–beige grosgrain ballerina flats–on the day
after she was scheduled to return from her trip to
Paris. He now considers them a special remem-
brance of her. Of his good friend, he said, "She was a
naturally beautiful woman inside and out and a lady
of great warmth, humility and compassion."

The auction was a huge success, raising
$3,258,750; an additional $2.5 million was raised
from catalog sales and fund-raising events. The Royal
Marsden Cancer Fund and the AIDS Crisis Trust in
London, and the Evelyn H. Lauder Breast Center of
Memorial Sloan-Kettering Cancer Center, the Har-

vard AIDS Institute and the AIDS Care Center of
The New York Hospital-Cornell Medical Center each
benefited from the gala receptions. Besides drawing a
symbolic line in her life between the past and the
present, Diana had achieved something that would
become her legacy: she legitimized her glamorous
image by using it for the benefit of others.

One of the best indications that Diana was
finally comfortable with herself and her
appearance was evident during the
summer of 1997 when she gave up going
from one designer to another looking for
"statement clothes." For three very important events–
the opening night of the National Ballet in London; a
Red Cross fund-raiser with Elizabeth Dole in Washington, D. C., for the victims of land mines; and one of her
last public appearances on July 1st, her 36th birthday,
where she was guest of honor at the Tate Gallery's
100th anniversary party in London–she had chosen to
wear the stunning designs of Jacques Azagury. The
designer presented Diana with the long beaded black
dress worn at the Tate Gallery as a birthday gift.

While in previous years Azagury often had to encourage Diana to try more daring styles, the tables had now turned. His silk georgette dress in pale blue with crystal beading, worn in June of 1997, was one of Diana's most revealing dresses. "The color caught her eye when she walked into the shop. She was slightly tan at the time and all those beads really brought out her eyes. I said, 'It's a little too low.' She said, 'No, it looks great.' She had a good eye and she knew immediately what she wanted. She came to me for a specific kind of dress. You couldn't sell her anything she didn't want. I don't think she wore low-cut dresses because she wanted to say, 'I've got a big bust'—it was the look of the moment. Cleavage-baring, figure-hugging dresses and short lengths were very much the fashion at the time."

Although Azagury worked with Diana over the course of twelve years, he never quite got used to seeing her appear in his Knightsbridge shop. "It was always very exciting to be with her. I'd always be a little bit nervous and she'd always say something funny to relax me." Diana, he said, was never difficult or demanding. "Whenever she came here from the Palace and other customers were in the shop, she'd say, 'It's okay, Jacques, finish with them.' Of course I wouldn't, but she always was polite enough to say that." While his clothes certainly looked as if they were made exclusively for her, Diana always selected styles from his current collections and never insisted they be taken off the line once she wore them. "It's not as if anyone else could look as beautiful," said the designer.

Out of all the Azagury designs that she wore (Diana owned eighteen of his dresses), the one that may well have showcased Diana's beauty best is one we will never see her wear. "It was a real 'movie-star' dress," said Azagury of the gown delivered to the Palace shortly before her death. "She was planning to wear it for a premiere in October. It was a full-length black bugle-beaded gown with thin shoulder straps, very low-cut in front with a high slit. It had a long train and she looked fantastic in it." Diana so loved the dress that during the final fitting, she told the designer about how she had learned to catwalk from Mario Testino during their *Vanity Fair* shoot. The Princess then gave an impromptu demonstration of her newfound skill. "She did this whole thing with the dress and the train to show me. She was completely natural and happy."

On the day Diana left for Paris, a package arrived from Kensington Palace addressed to the designer. There, in one large gold frame, were three photographs of Diana in the last three Azagury evening dresses she had worn. The simple inscription 'Love, Diana' was written in her hand beneath the images. "There will never be anybody to replace her. She was unbelievably genuine and completely unique," he said.

As the most enduring fashion icon of the modern age, Diana was the woman that millions of women around the world wanted to look at and look like. It is almost impossible to believe that we will never see another new look from Diana. And for her faithful admirers who took their fashion cues from her, there will never be another role model to replace her. She was equally captivating in ball gowns and blue jeans. In the end, Diana simply transcended fashion.

Diana chose a revealing beaded black dress for a gala dinner hosted by Chanel at the Tate Gallery in London, which she accessorized with an emerald and diamond choker (a wedding gift from the Queen) and matching earrings from Prince Charles. OPPOSITE, The Princess wanted something "movie-star-like" for a film premiere she was to attend in the fall of 1997. Jacques Azagury created this stunning dress with a plunging neckline, high-cut slit skirt and long train. She was, said Azagury, thrilled at the prospect of wearing it.

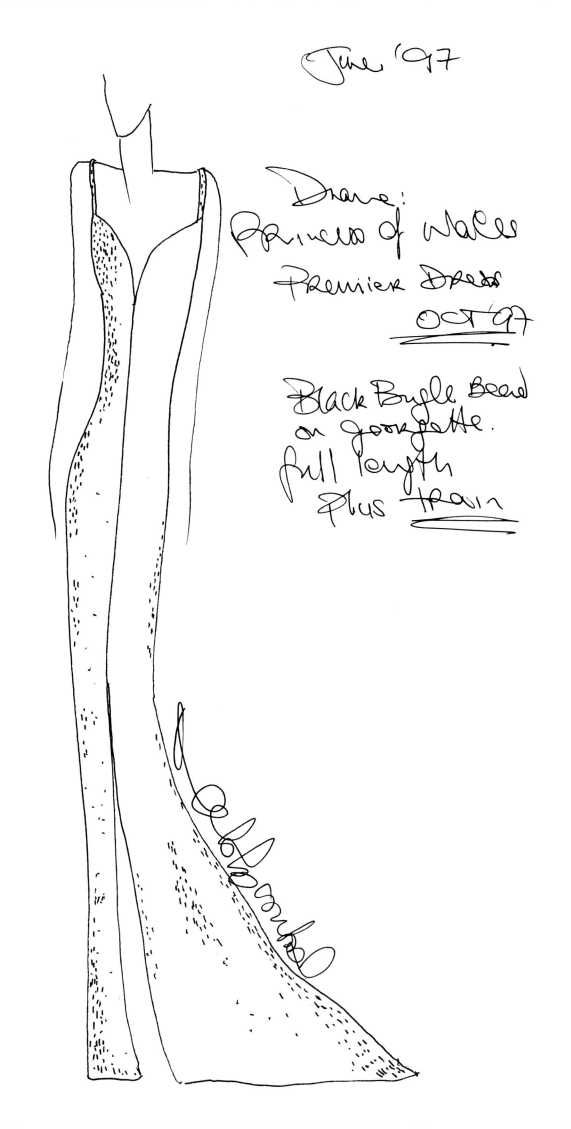

June '97

Diana:
Princess of Wales
Premier Dress
OCT 97

Black Bugle Bead
on Georgette.
Full Length
Plus Train

REMEMBERING
DIANA

Valentino, DESIGNER

"WHEN I met her at the very beginning, when she was married to Prince Charles, I immediately realized she was one of the most beautiful girls in the world. Year by year she became more sophisticated and sure of herself. Her style had changed, she was more aware of herself as a woman. Every designer was inspired by her. I did have the chance and honor to make several dresses for her. To me, she will always remain one of the most beautiful women and a friend who I sincerely miss."

Caroline Charles, DESIGNER

"WE WILL always miss her stylish and beautiful way of wearing clothes. She was the best ambassador of British fashion."

Christina Stambolian, DESIGNER

"SHE LOVED clothes. When she was confident and happy at the end of her life, she moved in a different way. She was so much more beautiful later on than she was in those first early years. In the end, she was a very modern girl."

Donald Campbell, DESIGNER

"SHE LOOKED best when she began wearing clothes from international designers. I think she had grown out of her 'Englishness' and to some extent, become international. She was a woman of the world. She wasn't going around dressed like the ladies she used to call 'the velvet headbands.'"

Oscar de la Renta, DESIGNER

"SHE HAD tremendous star quality. When she walked into a room, there wasn't anyone who didn't notice. She had the most beautiful smiling eyes I have ever seen."

Jacques Azagury, DESIGNER

"SHE WAS a very beautiful woman and the Princess of Wales. It was a real-life dynasty, really. There she was, this perfect looking woman, married to a Prince—with all the jewels, all the riches. It all seemed perfect for all those years until we knew what really happened. Beyond all that, she was such a lovely woman. The minute someone met her, they fell in love with her. She had the capacity to make you feel immediately at ease."

Philip Somerville, MILLINER

"I REMEMBER over the years going to see her and she would always walk to the car with me. At first, she would walk slightly stooped over. Then, suddenly in the last year she was straight, her legs were perfect and her figure was divine. She had what was every man's ideal of a woman's figure. She was a tall, elegant person but at the same time someone who was a great conversationalist and she was very much a man's woman."

David Sassoon, DESIGNER

"THERE WAS a tremendous change from the shy little girl who I initially dressed to this overtly glamorous woman. She was very charismatic as a person, not just because she was a princess. She had this caring quality. She had compassion. She suffered, too. She was a woman who showed her heart. She showed the pain of divorce; the jealousy of another woman being in the background—she was human. She was divine with her children. They always came first."

David Thomas, THE CROWN JEWELLER

"SHE WAS a princess. She had a style. She did everything with grace and charm."

"When she walked into a room, there wasn't anyone who didn't notice."

Geeta Sarin, DESIGNER
"ONE OF the things I loved about her was there were no barriers of culture–it was amazing. She wanted to dress appropriately as a sign of respect. When I showed her a sari, she asked, 'How do you drape six yards of fabric?' She thought they were beautiful. Then when I showed her my drawstring pants, she said, 'Good, something I can wear when I do my yoga.' The beautiful thing about her was she knew she was the most photographed woman in the world and she wanted to use that only for good, to help others."

Janet Filderman, SKINCARE EXPERT
"I THINK she had two main special gifts. One was her charisma which made you feel that you were the only person that she was at all interested in. It's a very rare thing when you can talk to someone and you think they are talking just to you and you alone. And then of course what she had was a sense of fun. I think she was a sort of beautiful butterfly. The butterfly gets more and more beautiful as a thing but then it doesn't last very long."

Marylou Luther, JOURNALIST
"THE FIRST time I saw her was at the tenth anniversary fashion show of Bruce Oldfield. At that point she was still very much 'Shy Di.' She did have a tendency to lower her head with her eyes peeking up as her cheeks reddened. She was wearing a backless lamé dress by Bruce and she was dancing. She loved to dance. When she came to Australia for the Bicentennial with the Prince in 1988, I could see at that time how well she was handling her public persona. Everyone was enchanted. Later that same year she presided over a reception at The State Apartments at Kensington Palace with Prince William at her side. I asked her if she often brought the Princes along on official duties and she told me she did because, she said, 'I want them to see what I do.'"

Bruce Oldfield, DESIGNER
"I MET her so many times and she was always such a laugh. We used to go for lunch, she liked to dish about everything. That's why she was such a laugh. She was always very, very good and very thoughtful with the people who worked for you. There would always be some sort of flowers and things that would come the next day after an event when she was happy with her frock. One of my fitters whose is retired now still gets Christmas cards –or did–even after I stopped getting one."

Richard Dalton, HAIRSTYLIST
"SHE HAD beautiful skin. I used to see her first thing in the morning when I was doing her hair and she was incredibly beautiful with that skin. It was that sort of English rose, the flush. She was comfortable in sweat pants and sneakers when she was doing her aerobics and she was just so incredibly glamorous in eveningwear.

Jimmy Choo, FOOTWEAR DESIGNER
"THE LAST time I went to Kensington Palace was before the Christie's auction. We were sitting cross-legged on the floor and she asked me if I was happy. I talked to her about Buddhism and I asked her if she meditated and she said she tried but it was too hard–something always distracted her."

Donna Karan, DESIGNER
"SHE WAS a symbol of what one meant when one spoke of icons. She took a role and created it with style and grace under enormous, enormous difficulty. She was a mentor to women and she set standards."

Elizabeth Emanuel, DESIGNER
"YOU EITHER have charisma or you don't. She had it. She was so brilliant with everyone–everyone just adored her. There are loads of movie stars and celebrities but there will be only one Diana."

ACKNOWLEDGMENTS

Diana was researched, written and produced over the course of nine months, during which time I have had the incredible good fortune to be the recipient of a great deal of support, love, friendship and sound advice from many sources. It is this positive energy and kindness that was a constant source of strength for me, particularly when I was feeling overwhelmed by the Herculean task of sifting through the mountain of images, hours of interview transcripts and mounds of information on Diana that went into creating this book.

With this project, my professional life has been blessed from the start. I am beyond grateful that my experience as a first-time author was with an editor as smart and sensitive as Leslie Stoker. Without her, there would be no book. Thank you, Leslie, for believing in *Diana* and in me with such conviction. I cannot adequately articulate just how much I greatly appreciate the creative freedom I enjoyed under your tutelage. Thank you for your faith in my words and in my vision of what *Diana* should be. Thank you for your respect, never-ending enthusiasm and your gentle guidance. My heartfelt thanks goes to Tom Klusaritz and everyone at GT Publishing for their support. And a huge thank you to a team of incredible people who put in the long hours and worked tirelessly to make *Diana* happen: copy editor Ruth Greenstein, designer Helene Silverman and editorial assistant Mimi O'Connor. To the team at Planned Television Arts— Margaret McAllister, Lisa Hollenberg, Kristin Conrad and Basia Irzyk: Your boundless enthusiasm has been wonderful and a sure sign of terrific things yet to come.

To my agents Gayle Benderoff and Deborah Geltman: Thank you for calling me that fateful weekend. If you hadn't, I don't know if this book would have happened. Thank you for believing in my idea and helping me shape it into a relevant, workable concept, for being so tenacious and for lending your ears every time I needed to talk and for finding *Diana* the right home.

This book is a true testament to the respect and affection for Diana of those in fashion who knew Diana best. I am extremely grateful to those people who chose to share their personal stories about the Princess with honesty and with great attention to detail. I know that in many cases, it was painful for some of them who agreed to be interviewed for this book to revisit bittersweet memories. My sincerest thanks goes to them and their gracious staffs: Simon Wilson, Donald Campbell, Caroline Charles and Amanda Evans, Jimmy Choo and Marsha Ilsey at Brower Lewis

PR, Richard Dalton, Janet Filderman, Stan Herman, Ann Jackson, Marylou Luther, Bruce Oldfield and Georgina Sinclair, Geeta Sarin and David Thomas. An extra special thank you to Jacques Azagury and Solange Azagury, Elizabeth Emanuel, David Sassoon, Christina Stambolian, Tomasz Starzewski and Sally Chiari and Philip Somerville and Dillon Wallwork, who not only spent a considerable amount of time with me being interviewed in London and New York but also graciously provided me with one-of-a-kind sketches for the book.

Thank you to those who generously provided much-needed assistance: Victoria Coode at Christie's in London, Janet Ozzard at the Paris Bureau of *Women's Wear Daily*, Edith-Marie Mead at Eleanor Lambert Ltd., Linda Gaunt and Rebecca Hirsch at Giorgio Armani (thank you for the stunning sketch!), Patrick O'Connell and Markus Ebner at KCD, Margaret Reilly-Muldoon, Lindy Woodhead, Lesley Exley, Annelise Matthew and Sayeed Ismail at The Chelsea Design Company, Alice Ryan at Oscar de la Renta, Patti Cohen at Donna Karan, and Pam Stein at Valentino.

I would also like to gratefully acknowledge the support so many colleagues offered. To Beth Arky at *TV Guide*, Lynne Dorsey at *Soap Opera Magazine*, Margaret Hayes at The Fashion Group International, Peter Antony at Calvin Klein, Pam McNally and Lauren Keller at Hachette Custom Publishing and Barrie Stern at F. Schumacher, thank you for allowing me to continue to do the work I do for you (and for the patience that required) while I wrote *Diana*. A special thank you to Freeman Gunter for providing me with a critical opportunity I so wanted that helped change the direction of my career. Thank you to those who found time in their busy schedules to offer support and advice: Kay Shadley, Sheri Lapidus, Lewis Taub, Maru Leon, Irena Notes, Jeannette Chang and Trica Jean-Baptiste. Thank you, Trica, for giving me that terrific opportunity with *New York Women in Communications* to talk about *Diana*. Peter Lyden, thank you for graciously offering to help bring an added sparkle to the book (there's always next time!). To Laura Messano of *Romance Classics*, thanks for letting me be a part of your "Day of Diana" and reach out to your audience in such a special way. A great big thank you to Betty Loiacono of The Norwich Inn and Spa and Anushka for generously offering me a respite from the outside world.

I owe a tremendous debt of gratitude to those who assisted me in my exhaustive search for the very best photographs of Diana. Thank you to Larry Schwartz of Archive Photos, Kellie McLaughlin and Julie Grahame at Retna, Robert Conway at Globe Photos and Kelli Souder at Sipa Press. And to my good pal George Smith, a million thanks for taking a such a flattering photograph!!

Nothing I have done in the past nine months would ever have gotten off the ground without the help of this intrepid group: To Michael Anderson, the one person who has kept my professional life in order for the last three years with extraordinary efficiency and good humor, I want to say that I know I'll have to someday, but I can't image functioning without you. (I tried once and it was an unmitigated disaster!). I know this isn't your life's work, but your dedication is unmatched by anyone I have ever worked with. Thank you for keeping Madeline Communications running so smoothly during the writing of this book, thank you for caring so much about everything you do for me but most of all thank you for your loyalty and your friendship. To Denise Limauro, thank you for stepping into the middle of this book and working on it with me as if it were your own. You are a first-rate editorial assistant with a rare designer's eye, excellent researcher and proofreader and a sensitive, caring friend. I'm so glad we met. Let's hear it for the Bay Shore girls! To Betsy O'Brien: Thank you for being the world's greatest intern! You got me through one *Style*-saturated summer and helped me start *Diana* on the right foot.

My trip to London to research this book was made infinitely more enjoyable thanks to the staff at The Basil Street Hotel (I hope your fax machine has recovered by now). I discovered in writing this book, it's the little things that can make–or break–your day. Having said that, I want to thank the gang at Starbucks and Mezza Luna in Eastchester for feeding my body and soothing my soul on a daily basis. David Jacobs at PAK MAIL, you were a godsend! And for all the people I have known in the course of my life who have said, 'You should write a book!' thanks for all that good karma that helped to make this incredible dream an even more incredible reality.

I am not the best person at maintaining any semblance of balance when I am working on something that is critically important to me–like this book. I want to say a huge thank you to my friends and family who have gently reminded me there is life outside of my tiny office. Thank you, Louisa Snape, for being the most caring, sympathetic and nuturing friend I could ever hope to have. And Lou, thank you for taking so much joy in seeing me fulfill a dream. Thank you, Karen Diamond for always being there for me these many, many years and for being an incredibly good listener. Thank you, Jennifer Bassey, for being caring enough to reach out to a stranger. Thank you, Lisa Hery, for being another set of eyes and ears at a moment's notice whenever I wanted a second opinion on anything. Thank you, Judy Simon, for whipping me into shape. Thank you to the Monday night group for their unflagging support. A very special thank you to Nancy Bernstein and Victoria Assumma who, not all that long ago, believed in me when I didn't have the strength to believe in myself. Your commitment to me has made a tremendous difference in my life. To Kathy Read and Barbara Tanguilig: Lots of love and appreciation for being there for Chris and me and staying true to your promises.

To Jim: Thank you for living with Diane and *Diana* all these many months, for listening to endless discussions about the book and for enduring hours upon hours of television coverage of the Princess that constantly filled our living room. There were times when I was "stark raving Diana" and you were able to make me laugh about the craziness of it all. To the Donovan family: The kindness you have shown me over the years has meant a great deal to me.

I certainly don't have one of the largest families, but I do have one of the best. To my brother Chris, sister-in-law Missy and Mr. Baby: Thank you for being an extremely enthusiastic cheering section (and mini-focus group) for the book and for everything I do. I love you more than words could ever say. Chris, you told me Mom sees everything we're doing and I know you're right. To my Nana: You are the strongest woman I know–I hope I've got lots of your DNA! And to the Stevensons who have "adopted" me: your constant thoughtfulness is a bright spot in my life.

I would like to end by thanking my mother, the one person who always believed in me. She would be thrilled to know that her nickname for me, "Dutchess," was the very same one that was given to Diana by her family. She instilled in me a love of fashion and great style and an unending fascination with strong, independent women. Perhaps that is why we loved to read and watch anything about Diana curled up together in our den. I will always remember the great fun we had shopping for clothes, jewelry and shoes that looked like our favorite things we had seen the Princess wear. We loved to laugh–we did that a lot. No matter what I did or said, she was always completely supportive of everything I ever attempted. For years we talked about me writing a book, about how exciting that would be. Unfortunately, I never got around to doing it while she was alive. I believe it is her spirit that has moved me to try things–like writing this book–that I never had the courage to do before. In my heart, I know she is still looking out for me and for that I will always be grateful.

SELECT BIBLIOGRAPHY

Anderson, Christopher. *Jackie After Jack*. New York: William Morrow and Company, Inc., 1998.

Bowles, Hamish. "Princess Diana Fashion Tribute." *Vogue*, November 1997, pp. 291-293.

Etherington-Smith, Meredith. "Diana Sequins Save Lives: The Inside Story of the Auction of the Century." *You Magazine* in *The Mail on Sunday*, 3 August 1997, pp. 2-32.

"Eye Scoop." *Women's Wear Daily*, 11 February 1997, p. 4.

Fincher, Jayne and Terry. *Debrett's Illustrated Fashion Guide, The Princess of Wales*. Great Britain: Webb & Bower Limited, 1989.

Lacey, Robert. *Princess*. New York: Times Books, 1982.

MacArthur, Brian. *Requiem Diana, Princess of Wales, 1961-1997*. New York: Arcade Publishing, 1997.

Morton, Andrew. *Diana, Her True Story–In Her Own Words*. New York: Simon & Schuster, 1997.

Seward, Ingrid. *Diana: An Intimate Portrait*. Chicago: Contemporary Books, 1997.

Tilberis, Liz. *No Time To Die*. New York: Little, Brown and Company, 1998.

PHOTO CREDITS

Front cover: Kim Knott/Camera Press/Retna
Spine: Reuters/Mike Theiler/Archive Photos
Back cover: Press Association/Archive Photos, Express Newspaper/Archive Photos, Reuters/Jose Manuel/Archive Photos

Page 6: P.A. News/Archive Photos. 11: By kind permission, Giorgio Armani. 12, 13: Snowdon/Camera Press/Retna. 14,15: Terence Donovan /Camera Press/Retna. 16,17: Alpha/Globe Photos. 20: D. Chancellor/Alpha/GlobePhotos. 21L: Archive Photos/Press Association. 21C: D. Chancellor/Alpha/Globe Photos. 21R: Camera Press/Retna. 23: Tony Drabble/Globe Photos. 24: Express Newspapers/Archive Photos. 25T: Camera Press/Globe Photos. 25B: Camera Press/Globe Photos. 26: Bennett/Camera Press/Globe Photos. 27: By kind permission, David Sassoon. 29: Camera Press/Globe Photos. 30: Archive Photos. 32: Archive Photos/Express Newspapers. 34: Sipa Press. 35L: Anwar Hussein/Retna. 35R: Richard Young/Retna. 37: Archive Photos/Express Newspapers. 39BL: Anwar Hussein/Sipa Press. 39TR: Alpha/Globe Photos. 40L: Archive Photos. 40R: Anwar Hussein/Sipa Press. 41: Anwar Hussein/Sipa Press. 43: Express Newspapers/Archive Photos. 44: All Action/Retna. 45: Alpha/Globe Photos. 47: Express Newspapers/Archive Photos. 49: Reuters/Peter Jones/Archive Photos. 51: Jim Bennett /Alpha/Globe Photos. 52: Glenn Harvey/Retna. 53: By kind permission, Elizabeth Emanuel. 54: Ron Sachs/CNP/Archive Photos. 55: Peter Heimsath/CNP/Archive Photos. 56: Reuters/Ronald Reagan Presidential Library/Archive Photos. 59: Express Newspapers/Archive Photos. 60T: Pictorial Parade/Archive Photos. 60C: Monitor/Archive Photos. 60B: Cherruault/Sipa Press. 61: Popperfoto/Archive Photos. 62T: Harvey/Stills /Retna. 62B: Harvey/Retna. 63: Sipa Press. 65: Archive Photos/Express Newspapers. 67: By kind permission, Philip Somerville. 68: Imapress /Cotteau/Archive Photos. 69, 70: By kind permission, Philip Somerville. 71T: Harvey/Stills/Retna. 71B: Harvey/Retna. 72L: Harvey/Stills/Retna. 72R: By kind permission, Philip Somerville. 74: By kind permision, Philip Somerville. 75: Archive Photos/Express News. 76T: Harvey/Stills /Retna. 76B: Hussein/All Action/Retna. 77: Harvey/Stills/Retna. 78: Archive Photos. 80: Harvey/Stills/Retna. 81: By kind permission, Tomasz Starzewski. 82: Arnal/Stills/Retna. 83: Archive Photos/Express News. 84L: D. Chancellor/Alpha/Globe Photos. 84R: Melia/Retna. 85: Reuters /Andew Wong/Archive Photos. 86, 87, 88, 91, 92: Express Newspapers/Archive Photos. 93: D. Chancellor/Alpha/Globe Photos. 94: Archive Photos/Express Newspapers. 97: Archive Photos/Pappix U.K. 98: By kind permission, Christina Stambolian. 100: Alpha/Globe Photos. 101: By kind permission, Christina Stambolian. 103, 105: Archive Photos/Press Association. 106: Archive Photos. 107: Big Pictures/Archive News Photos. 108: Archive Photos. 109: Anwar Hussein/All Action/Retna. 110: Archive Photos/Express Newspapers. 112: Press Association/Archive Photos. 113: Archive News Photos/Press Association. 114: P.A. News/Archive Photos. 115: Express Newspapers /Archive Photos. 117: All Action/Retna. 118, 119: D. Chancellor/Alpha/Globe Photos. 120: Archive Photos/Press Association. 121: Reuters/Olson/Archive Photos. 122: Finn/Alpha/Globe Photos. 123: R. Chambury/Alpha/Globe Photos. 124: Reuters/M. Theiler/Archive Photos. 125: Reuters/S. Jaffe/Archive Photos. 126: Reuters/S. Jaffe/Archive Photos. 128: Archive News Photos/Press Association. 131: Reuters/D. Pollard/Archive Photos. 133: Cherruault/Sipa Press. 134L: Express Newspapers/Archive Photos. 134R: Cherruault/Sipa Press. 137: LRC/Sipa Press. 138: Meigneux/SANDA /Sipa Press. 139: Reuters/Jose Manuel/Archive Photos. 140: Reuters/Mike Segar/Archive Photos. 141: Alpha/Globe Photos. 142: Reuters/Brad Rickerby/Archive Photos. 143T, R, B: Camera Press/Retna. 143L: Snowdon/Camera Press/Retna.145: Schaeffer/CNP/Archive Photos. 146: D. Bennett/Alpha/Globe Photos. 148: Reuters/Michael Crabtree/Archive Photos. 149: By kind permission, Jacques Azagury. 151: Express Newspapers/Archive Photos. 152: Reuters/Ian Waldie/Archive Photos. 154, 155: Express Newspapers / Archive Photos.